THE BERGDAHL EXCHANGE: IMPLICATIONS FOR U.S. NATIONAL SECURITY AND THE FIGHT AGAINST TERRORISM

JOINT HEARING

BEFORE THE

SUBCOMMITTEE ON TERRORISM, NONPROLIFERATION, AND TRADE

AND THE

SUBCOMMITTEE ON THE MIDDLE EAST AND NORTH AFRICA

OF THE

COMMITTEE ON FOREIGN AFFAIRS HOUSE OF REPRESENTATIVES

ONE HUNDRED THIRTEENTH CONGRESS

SECOND SESSION

JUNE 18, 2014

Serial No. 113–158

Printed for the use of the Committee on Foreign Affairs

Available via the World Wide Web: http://www.foreignaffairs.house.gov/ or
http://www.gpo.gov/fdsys/

U.S. GOVERNMENT PRINTING OFFICE

88–387PDF   WASHINGTON : 2014

For sale by the Superintendent of Documents, U.S. Government Printing Office
Internet: bookstore.gpo.gov   Phone: toll free (866) 512–1800; DC area (202) 512–1800
Fax: (202) 512–2104   Mail: Stop IDCC, Washington, DC 20402–0001

COMMITTEE ON FOREIGN AFFAIRS

(III)

CONTENTS

THE BERGDAHL EXCHANGE: IMPLICATIONS FOR U.S. NATIONAL SECURITY AND THE FIGHT AGAINST TERRORISM

WEDNESDAY, JUNE 18, 2014

House of Representatives,
Subcommittee on Terrorism, Nonproliferation, and Trade
AND
Subcommittee on the Middle East and North Africa,
Committee on Foreign Affairs,
Washington, DC.

The committees met, pursuant to notice, at 2 o'clock p.m., in room 2172 Rayburn House Office Building, Hon. Ted Poe (chairman of the subcommittee) presiding.

Mr. POE. The subcommittee will come to order. Without objection all members will have 5 days to submit statements, questions, and extraneous materials for the record subject to the length limitation in the rules.

The purpose of this hearing is to hear more about Sergeant Bowe Bergdahl and his exchange for five terrorist prisoners from Guantanamo Bay. Let's hope that the Bergdahl negotiators are not the same ones currently negotiating with Iran over nuclear weapons.

Be that as it may, releasing five senior Taliban commanders may put the lives of our senior service members and Americans around the world at risk. One of the five detainees was a Deputy Chief of the Taliban's Intelligence Service. One detainee fought alongside al-Qaeda as a Taliban Military General. Another was a Senior Commander wanted by the United Nations for war crimes and worked closely with al-Qaeda and their affiliates. In fact, he led an attack with al-Qaeda the day before 9/11. Al-Qaeda called this attack an important part of the 9/11 total strategy. And still another was a close confidante of Taliban Leader Mullah Omar.

The terms of the release to Qatar are quite disturbing. They may help out the Taliban while they are in Qatar, and it's very likely that all of them will end up fighting alongside the Taliban in Afghanistan later in the year. That will be about the time United States forces will be leaving and the Afghans will be on their own.

It appears that recent law that was signed by the President was violated in this secret deal. This law, among other things, requires two things; that the administration must notify Congress 30 days before releasing Guantanamo Bay detainees. And, second, the administration has to specifically tell Congress how releasing each terrorist is in the national security interest of the United States.

The administration did neither. Plus, it has been the policy of the United States not to negotiate with terrorists, and this seems to also have been violated.

The Haqqani Network are the ones who held Sergeant Bergdahl. It's a designated foreign terrorist organization according to the United States State Department and has killed countless Americans and Afghan soldiers. It maintains close ties with al-Qaeda and it's the most dangerous terrorist group fighting in Afghanistan.

It doesn't matter that Qatar acted as a go-between the United States because it did involve negotiating with terrorists in the Haqqani Network. This raises another concern close to home in Texas.

One of my constituents, Victor Lovelady, was taken hostage during the terrorist attack on an Algerian gas facility in January 2013, an event that many Americans have forgotten. He was captured after he hid some of his coworkers in a space in the refinery. The terrorists never found the coworkers and they eventually escaped alive.

It's been reported that the hostage takers wanted to trade those three American hostages at the facility, including Victor, for two convicted terrorists in the United States custody. Victor's brother, Michael, and his daughter, Erin, wrote to me recently to say that they were told by our Government during the attack that the United States does not negotiate with terrorists. Victor was later killed.

I ask for unanimous consent that the letters be made part of the record. So ordered.

The Bergdahl release troubled them, and rightly so. Victor's daughter wrote to me in this letter, ''The question that continues to come to mind is what makes one American life more important than another? And if we're going to negotiate for one, why would we not negotiate for everybody?'' I cannot answer that question, and I really do not know what the United States' current policy is on negotiating with terrorists. Maybe we will find out.

Negotiating with a designated terrorist organization like we did with the Haqqani Network is unprecedented. Department of Defense says it will hold Sergeant Bergdahl accountable for his actions; however, National Security Advisor Susan Rice has said that Sergeant Bergdahl has served with honor and distinction. Once again, this hearing will shed more light on that issue. One of our witnesses today served with Sergeant Bergdahl and he will discuss Bergdahl's disappearance.

Secretary of Defense Chuck Hagel is on record stating that he was not aware of any United States soldier who lost their life in search for Sergeant Bergdahl. The family of one of those brave Americans who gave his life, Lieutenant Darryn Andrews, is here today to set the record straight. He earned a Silver Star for his actions which included protecting his brothers in arms and taking the brunt of the Taliban rocket-propelled grenade which ultimately took his life. Darryn left behind a pregnant wife and a young son at the time of his death.

So, today we have witnesses who can tell us what else happened in eastern Afghanistan in 2009, those who have suffered as a result, and what this so called deal may mean for Afghanistan and the United States going forward.

I yield back my time, and I will now recognize the ranking member from California, Mr. Sherman, for 5 minutes.

Mr. SHERMAN. Thank you. Mr. Andrews. We know that you are the father of Darryn Andrews, Second Lieutenant who gave his life for his country. We cannot thank you enough for your family's sacrifice. We salute Darryn's courage.

I would also like to thank you, Specialist Full for your service to our country. Mr. Waltz is a Senior National Security Fellow at the New America Foundation who commanded Special Forces in eastern Afghanistan. Thank you for your service. And Dr. Jacobson, thank you for your 20 years of service in the military, including your deployment to Afghanistan.

First, as to a preliminary issue on Iraq, let me point out that we do not have forces in Iraq. We do not have a Status of Forces Agreement with Iraq. It was President Bush that installed al-Maliki as Prime Minister of Iraq in 2006, and the misgovernance of Prime Minister Maliki is directly responsible for the violence taking place in that country today. It should not be surprising that Maliki refused to enter a Status of Forces Agreement with the United States under President Obama. He refused to enter a long-term Status of Forces Agreement with President Bush, the man who, in effect, allowed him to take power.

As to releases from Guantanamo, while we're focusing today on five Guantanamo prisoners being released, President Bush released over 500 prisoners from Guantanamo. Most of them were dangerous. Over 100 of them we know are fighting us on the battlefield and we know where. Most of the others are fighting against us, as well. We just can't pinpoint where they are located. And what did we get for the 500 that President Bush released? Absolutely nothing except thank you notes from their native countries.

As to Section 1035 D of the National Defense Authorization Act, the President has filed a report. Members of this committee can go read it. It is in depth. It is arguably late as many reports to Congress are.

Keep in mind that we have to construe Section 1035 D so as to avoid constitutional questions; therefore, it has been and should be interpreted not to apply in this circumstance, particularly in a circumstance involving a prisoner exchange.

Keep in mind that the last Republican Attorney General of the United States, Michael Mirkasey, stated that ''This code section is unconstitutional to the extent it acts to prevent a prisoner exchange.''

Now, I would have preferred if President Obama had, indeed, conferred with leaders of Congress. I'm glad to see he is conferring with congressional leaders about what to do in Iraq. America is strongest when our President views Members of Congress as a source of counsel and input, not persons to be notified only when the notification is compelled by a constitutionally valid statute.

And I will point out that Members of Congress, leaders of Congress can keep a secret. Some 16 congressional leaders knew that we had ascertained the hiding place of Osama bin Laden, and that information did not leak.

As to negotiating with terrorists, it's a nice phrase that we don't do it. The fact is, we do it all the time. The Bush administration negotiated with every single terrorist regime in the world. We identified five state sponsors of terrorism, and the Bush administration negotiated with Cuba, Iran, Sudan, Syria, and North Korea. The Bush administration paid an al-Qaeda affiliate a ransom for the release of Martin and Gracia Burnham. Secretary of State Colin Powell designated the Afghan Taliban as an organization authorized for legal authorization.

Now, it is said that because we paid a price for the release of Bergdahl that this put terrorists around the world on notice of a fact they somehow didn't know before, and that is that America cares about those who are detained. A walk through the halls of this building shows the POW flags from the Vietnam War. Everyone in the world knows that we care about our detainees. There are resolutions introduced by Republican members available to anyone on the Internet that show that we regard the release of Sergeant Bergdahl as an important national objective.

Bringing our prisoners home is important to America. The enemy already knows that, and we know it, as well. And I yield back.

Mr. POE. The gentleman yields back. For the information of the committees, we are in a series of votes. The Chair plans to hear the opening statements of all the members and then come back for the testimony after the vote.

The Chair now recognizes the ranking member of the Middle East Subcommittee, chairman. You're not the ranking member, although——

Ms. ROS-LEHTINEN. It's good enough. Thank you.

Mr. POE [continuing]. Mr. Sherman thinks you should be.

Ms. ROS-LEHTINEN. Thank you very much.

Mr. POE. For 5 minutes, thank you.

Ms. ROS-LEHTINEN. Thank you. I thank the witnesses for being with us, especially Mr. Andrews whose son Darryn Deen was killed in Afghanistan in 2009, and Mr. Full, and Mr. Waltz, thank you for your service. Mr. Andrews, I cannot imagine what it would feel like to lose a child in the service of our nation, but as a stepmother of a U.S. Marine Aviator who served in Iraq, and a mother-in-law to another Marine Aviator who served in both Iraq and Afghanistan, I know the sleepless nights and the constant worry that parents face when their child or loved ones are constantly in harm's way.

Our country owes our brave men and women who have served and who have earned our gratitude a debt that can never be repaid, but it must start with being completely forthcoming with them.

In late 2011, while I was chair of the House Foreign Affairs Committee, the administration gathered the chairmen and the ranking members of the pertinent national security committees, as well as congressional leaderships to brief us on a potential prisoner swap of Taliban terrorists for Sergeant Bowe Bergdahl. And although the meeting was classified, news reports from just earlier this month indicate that the administration had a team of officials from the National Security Council, Pentagon, State Department, CIA, Director of National Intelligence present the administration's plan to us.

At the time of the briefing, using all available information given to me, I was adamantly opposed to the proposed swap, I said so at the meeting as did many of our colleagues. My opinion has not changed as more information has been revealed.

I opposed the swap not because I did not want to bring Bowe home. It's important to have him home and out of the hands of the Taliban. I opposed the swap because the proposal would have resulted in a huge coup for the Taliban, would have benefitted them, jeopardized the safety and security of our brave men and women in uniform, and compromised our national security interest.

With so many of our colleagues expressing our disapproval of the swap, the administration seemed to have gotten the message and dropped its exchange plan, or so we thought. Then earlier this month, I like the rest of my congressional colleagues and the American public read the news that the administration had swapped five Taliban commanders for the Sergeant. Despite his promises to notify Congress, not to mention its legal authority to do so, the administration kept the deal secret and acted unilaterally. The deal is precisely the reason for the legal mandate that Congress be given 30 days notice because the administration has a proven track record of overstepping and abusing its authority.

As we've already seen, the Taliban used this to its benefit using the video tape of the exchange as propaganda, and as a recruitment video. And it has only emboldened them further. Not only that, but despite the agreement with the Government of Qatar, which by the way is only for 1 year, to supervise these five Taliban high-level operatives, there are no assurances that they won't be back in the fight in short order and orchestrating attacks from their lavish new headquarters in Doha.

The fact that we are placing our hopes in Qatar, a country that has been full throated in its support for the Muslim Brotherhood, especially in Egypt where Qatar's support for the Brotherhood actively worked against our interest in seeing a Democratic transition there, will likely further or strain our already damaged ties with our traditional partners in the Gulf.

This may have serious implications for our national security objectives, especially as it relates to our efforts in Iran. But this swap is more than just Bowe Bergdahl or the Taliban, it's about U.S. national security, the safety of our men and women in uniform, and it's about the administration's disregard for the law and the contempt it holds for its obligations to Congress.

The administration's deal to swap five senior Taliban officials for the Sergeant has far-reaching implications. Negotiating and ultimately forging a deal with Taliban terrorists unnecessarily endangers all of the service men and women who are operating in war zones right now that these five senior Taliban operatives are likely to rejoin the fight. And it also inspires the Taliban and other terrorist groups to conduct abductions of our armed forces personnel, as we have already seen one Taliban commander admit that the Taliban is now encouraged by the results of the Bergdahl trade.

Then, of course, there are questions of the legality of the administration's unilateral decision, and the frustration level and lack of trust that Congress has with the administration as a result of this swap. There are many, many unanswered questions, Mr. Chairman, the administration still needs to answer, but for today it's important that we have the opportunity to hear from some of the people and how this decision has impacted them personally, those who served in Afghanistan fighting side by side with a fellow soldier, those service men and women who may have been placed even further in harm's way as a result of this exchange, and those who lost a loved one in Afghanistan, they deserve to be heard, and they deserve the truth.

Thank you, Mr. Chairman, for the time.

Mr. POE. Thank the gentle lady for yielding back her time.

The Chair recognizes the ranking member of the Middle East Subcommittee, Mr. Deutch, from Florida for 5 minutes.

Mr. DEUTCH. Thank you, Chairman Poe and Ranking Member Sherman.

To our witnesses, thanks for appearing today. Mr. Andrews, I join with my colleagues in telling you that words will never be enough to express our gratitude for your son, your family for making the ultimate sacrifice for this country. I appreciate your being here today, and will forever be grateful to Darryn for his courageous service to our nation.

Mr. Full, we're deeply grateful for your honorable service to this country. And Mr. Waltz, Mr. Jacobson, thank you for being here and for your years of service.

We all know that there are substantial questions surrounding the disappearance of Sergeant Bergdahl and the subsequent decision to exchange the Taliban Five for his release. It may take months before we know for sure what transpired in the days and weeks leading up to the disappearance of Army Sergeant Bowe Bergdahl. Was he suffering from psychological trauma? Was he AWOL? Was he a deserter? The Army investigation has begun and rest assured answers to these questions will come to light and the Army will take whatever action it deems appropriate.

I'm a bit perplexed when some Members of Congress have already decided the facts of this case. We have a solemn obligation to leave no American soldier behind. And when the opportunity to get an American soldier back from the enemy presents itself, we take it. This country has a long history of getting American servicemen back through prisoner exchanges because we promised the men and women, when they signed up bravely to serve their country, that we would do everything that we can to protect them and to ensure that they return home.

Some of my colleagues have apparently concluded now how Sergeant Bergdahl's status should be treated, how the facts should be resolved. And that perhaps one concludes that he be left with the Taliban. So, I would ask what kind of military court is it, what kind of military court of justice do we have where Members of Congress play the role of judge and jury, find someone guilty, and leave it to the Taliban to carry out the punishment?

We have every right to question why Congress wasn't consulted and notified of this deal. I believe that was a mistake, but I would simply caution against prejudging the facts of this case. What message are we sending our troops if we don't do everything that we can to retrieve an American soldier that the Army has officially declared missing and captured? You can have a debate over whether the price for Sergeant Bergdahl was too high, and it's an appropriate debate to have, but we should also be reminded of the 532 Guantanamo Bay detainees who were transferred before this President came to office. Where was the outrage then?

There are those who have suggested that the administration has politicized this deal. I would simply point out that many members of this Congress who are now saying that they oppose this deal supported the very idea of a prisoner exchange and were urging the administration to do more to secure the release of Sergeant Bergdahl.

Turning back to our witness, Mr. Andrews, there is nothing that we can say to take away the pain of losing a child, and I'd like again to offer my sincerest gratitude for Darryn's honorable service to his country. I thank you, Mr. Full, I thank you for your service, and all of the witnesses for your commitment to protecting this nation. I appreciate the opportunity to hear from all of you today, and I yield back.

Mr. POE. I appreciate the gentleman yielding back some of his time.

The Chair will now recognize the individual members for 1 minute of their opening statements. Mr. Chabot from Ohio is recognized for 1 minute.

Mr. CHABOT. Thank you. Like many of my colleagues and most constituents I talk with, I'm very troubled with the administration's insistence that the deal made to free five Taliban leaders in exchange for Sergeant Bergdahl was the best deal we could get.

The Washington Post reports that among the Taliban Five are the former Taliban Interior Minister who was known to have close ties to Osama Bin Laden, a former Taliban Army Chief of Staff who along with another of the freed Taliban is thought to have been present when CIA Officer Johnny Spam was killed back in 2001, and two Taliban operatives who work closely with al-Qaeda, notably Mohammad Nabi Omari, whose case file says is "one of the most significant former Taliban leaders detained" at Guantanamo Bay.

Now, I don't know how many of my colleagues have had the opportunity to visit our facility in Guantanamo Bay and look into the eyes of those who were involved in the killing of so many. I've been there three times. As much as I'd like to think that they've learned the error of their ways and want nothing more than to spend a quiet life with their families in Doha, I'm afraid you'd have to put me down in the skeptical, very skeptical column. I yield back.

Mr. POE. The gentleman yields back. The Chair will hear the testimony or the opening statement of one more member, and then we'll hear the rest of them after the vote.

Mr. Cicilline from Rhode Island is recognized for 1 minute.

Mr. CICILLINE. Thank you, Mr. Chairman. I thank you and Ranking Members Deutch and Sherman for holding today's hearing. I want to thank all of the witnesses, especially Mr. Andrews and Specialist Full for their services and for your willingness to share your very personal stories with us today. Words can never adequately provide comfort to you, Mr. Andrews, and to your family, nor can words convey the deep gratitude of our entire nation for the service of your son.

It's important that we take time today and in the weeks and months ahead to diligently, and thoroughly, and dispassionately examine the details surrounding the exchange of several high-value prisoners from the detention facility at Guantanamo Bay for the return of Sergeant Bowe Bergdahl.

We should never lose sight of the long-held American tradition that we'll do everything possible to secure the release of an American service member. I'm hopeful that today's hearing will highlight ways in which the administration and Congress can work together to protect the safety of our armed forces and insure the security of our country.

I look forward to hearing from the witnesses and gaining greater clarity regarding the circumstances surrounding the exchange of Sergeant Bergdahl.

And, finally, I hope this hearing will serve as a reminder to all of us that we must stay focused on ending American involvement in Afghanistan, and insuring the safe return of our fellow Americans serving there.

Thank you, and I yield back.

Mr. POE. The gentleman from Rhode Island yields back. The Chair will be in recess for 15 minutes, and we'll continue with opening statements, then testimony of our witnesses.

[Recess.]

Mr. POE. The subcommittee will come to order. The Chair recognizes the gentleman from Illinois, Mr. Kinzinger, for 1 minute.

Mr. KINZINGER. Thank you, Mr. Chairman. It's fun listening to I think the strategy session across the aisle was hey, what are going to do? Well, let's blame Bush. It seemed to have worked for the last 6 years, so it's going to be an interesting hearing.

I just want to say first off, thank you to the witnesses for being here. You know, when I went through survival training I was told your country will never leave you behind. I think it's very important to note that there was kind of a mutual understanding that your country will never leave you behind, if you never leave your country behind. And then, secondly, there was a mutual understanding that there can be a cost that is too great to pay. Your country promised to always search for you, they promised to move Heaven and Earth to come get you, but I was never in survival training promised that my country would release some of the five biggest enemies of the United States and the people that we've tried to bring freedom to in exchange. So, I'm interested to hear what everybody's thoughts is on why this happened, and some of the things surrounding this. I only have a minute, so I want to thank the chairman and yield back.

Mr. POE. The gentleman yields back. The Chair recognizes the gentle lady from Florida, Ms. Frankel, for 1 minute. I know you ran back.

Ms. FRANKEL. Catch my breath. Well, thank you, and thank you, gentlemen for all being here. Mr. Andrews, my heart breaks for you, and to the gentlemen, I thank you for your service.

I want to give a little different—my own personal perspective. My own son has served both in Iraq and Afghanistan as a United

States Marine. I'm very proud of that. He is home. But I will tell you this, when he went off to war I, of course, like probably most parents not only feared he would not come home alive, or that he would come home very maimed; but for me, my biggest worry was that he would be taken as a prisoner of war, tortured, put in a cage. It was just unimaginable. And that's why I believe so strongly in the U.S. military principle that we should leave no man or woman behind. It maintains confidence, it maintains order.

When we send our young men and women off to war, they should know we have their backs. We will do everything possible to bring them home. Thank you, again, for your service and, sir, for your loss.

Mr. POE. The Chair thanks the gentlewoman. The Chair recognizes the gentleman from Arkansas, Mr. Cotton, for 1 minute.

Mr. COTTON. Five years ago today I was a captain in the United States Army in Laughman Province so I think I will take the prerogative to speak on behalf of the soldiers who served in Afghanistan. I find it offensive and insulting that this administration, up to and including the President, would cite the principle of leaving no man behind to justify this action.

Every day in Ranger School we recited the Ranger Creed, that I will never leave a fallen comrade. You know who didn't leave a fallen comrade, Cody Full, Darryn Andrews, or all of the soldiers who went after him in the weeks and the months after his disappearance knowing that he had deserted.

When we made those promises to each other, we didn't promise that we would exchange five stone-cold Taliban killers for each other, nor would any soldier want that to happen. Would we exchange Khalid Sheik Mohammed? Deputy National Security Advisor Tony Blinken said directly to me that we would not.

Finally, I want to say something to the anonymous sources in the President's administration for disparaging the service of the 2nd Platoon and Blackfoot Company. Show yourself, speak your own name, have the courage of your convictions. And if you don't, shut up and stand back and thank these men for their service.

Mr. POE. The Chair recognizes the gentleman from Florida, Mr. DeSantis, for 1 minute.

Mr. DESANTIS. Thank you, Mr. Chairman.

I'm hearing my colleagues on the other side talking about oh, don't politicize this, but then blame Bush or whatever. It seems to me that, you know, the President politicized this when he had a White House Rose Garden ceremony for Mr. Bergdahl's parents.

I'm going to ask Mr. Andrews, and I'd like to know whether any of the people who served honorably and were killed in action were given the courtesy of a Rose Garden ceremony at the White House? I think the answer to that is probably no.

The bottom line here is either what the President did benefitted the security of the United States, or it did not. I believe it did not, and I think that this was something that the American people disagree with. And I see that many of my colleagues on the other side of the aisle are looking to essentially run interference for the administration by blaming previous Presidents. That doesn't cut it. Let's deal with this issue as its own, and I yield back.

Mr. POE. The Chair recognizes the gentleman from Virginia, Mr. Connolly, for 1 minute.

Mr. CONNOLLY. Thank you, Mr. Chairman. And, Mr. Andrews, my deepest sympathy to you and your family. That may be your wife behind you? There aren't any words to express the terrible sense of loss you must experience. And I've had friends have similar losses and my heart goes out to you. Thank you for being here today.

We're here today to examine the decision to exchange Sergeant Bergdahl, a soldier held in captivity for 5 years, for five detainees in Guantanamo. Now, it's easy to yield to the temptation to decide that Mr. Bergdahl did not serve his country. I would caution my colleagues, this isn't a partisan affair. This is about somebody's service, and we should withhold judgment on the quality and nature of that service until the facts are known. The benefit of the doubt belongs to Mr. Bergdahl pending that. It is not for Congress in advance to decide somebody's status before we justify leaving no one behind. So, I'm interested in this hearing. I'm interested in the facts, and I plead with my colleagues on both sides of the aisle this one time to let us resist the temptation of partisanship. Thank you, Mr. Chairman.

Mr. POE. The Chair recognizes the gentleman from North Carolina, Mr. Meadows, for 1 minute.

Mr. MEADOWS. Thank you, Mr. Chairman. I recently returned from Guantanamo, and got to look in the eyes of many of the detainees that are there. Make no mistake, the ones that we released, are in no comparison to the 400 or 500 that have been released prior. These men were a danger to the ones who guarded them, so dangerous that we can't even identify those who do guard them for their own protection.

They are not choir boys, but I will assure you they are singing a song. It is a death march for those men and women who will come in their way in the future, and the cost in my opinion was way too high to release the Taliban Five in exchange for this. And with that, I yield back.

Mr. POE. The gentleman yields back his time. The Chair recognizes the gentlemen from Texas, Mr. Weber, for 1 minute.

Mr. WEBER. Thank you, Mr. Chairman. My colleague is correct, this is not a partisan affair. This is the Committee of Foreign Affairs, and that it is, it is a foreign affair. And the President is charged with negotiating on our behalf, unfortunately. I hope that we come to the conclusion to implore this President, Mr. President, stop negotiating on our behalf, please.

Some would say that in military terms what the President did, we got one conventional weapon, some would say a dud. They got five nuclear weapons. Maybe we need to come to the conclusion to send a letter to the President, please, Mr. President, stop negotiating for us.

As to the Andrews, as Abraham Lincoln said in a letter to Mrs. Bixby, ''There's no words that we can express to you but to generally relate our sincere appreciation for your sacrifice.''

Thank you very much. I yield back.

Mr. POE. The gentleman yields back. The Chair recognizes the gentleman from California, Mr. Rohrabacher, for 1 minute.

Mr. ROHRABACHER. Thank you very much. President Obama has put American military personnel, U.S. diplomatic personnel, and yes, even American businessmen and tourists at risk by releasing five terrorist leaders in exchange for a captured American. We have given terrorists the incentive to capture and hold hostages more and more.

I would say that what we have to realize is that our President has just made a decision that will result in our country and our people being less safe than had he not made that decision. And, yes, President Bush released 500 Taliban that had been held in GITMO, but let me note, he did not make a deal for them. He did a survey to find out if they were the least threatening of those people who were being held. Had he done a deal for them, we would be condemning him, as well.

The fact is, this was an exchange, a specific exchange, a quid pro quo that will do nothing but encourage terrorists around the world to seek other hostages to make similar deals.

Our President has done a great disservice to those who defend us, as well as to the people of the United States. He's put us at risk.

Mr. POE. The gentleman yields back his time. The Chair recognizes the gentleman from South Carolina, Mr. Wilson, for 1 minute.

Mr. WILSON. Thank you, Mr. Chairman. And, Mr. and Mrs. Andrews, thank you so much for your family's service. Specialist Full, thank you for your service. It's very personal to me. My two older sons served in Iraq, my third son served in Egypt, and my fourth son just returned from his service in Afghanistan, so I truly have a great appreciation of the commitment of military families, service members, or veterans. And the President has disrespected all of them by releasing five Taliban. The response was mass murder in Pakistan. There were two attacks on the airport there in Karachi, dozens of people were murdered. Also, Shiite pilgrims were murdered just last week. The response is very, very clear.

And, in fact, we found out that one of the Taliban leaders said how much he appreciated the release, the pardon of one of the particular Taliban Five who is the equivalent of 10,000 Taliban fighters. This is serious. The President has put the American people at risk. Thank you for being here.

Mr. POE. Does any other member wish to be recognized for opening statement? Seeing none, the Chair will go into the statements of the witnesses. Without objection, all the witnesses' prepared statements will be made part of the record. I ask that each witness please keep your presentation to no more than 5 minutes. When you see the red light come on that means stop.

You're welcome to summarize your prepared statements if you need to. Witnesses are also advised that, as usual, testimony provided to the subcommittee is subject to the False Statements Act under 18 USC Section 1001; and, thus, any deliberate misrepresentation or concealment of material information is punishable by law.

I'll introduce each of the witnesses, and then we'll allow them to testify in the order that they are seated. Mr. Andy Andrews is the father of the fallen Second Lieutenant Darryn Andrews who was reportedly killed while on mission to look for Sergeant Bergdahl.

He is joined by his wife, Sandra Andrews, who is seated directly behind him, and she is wearing the dog tags of her son.

Mr. Andrews, I know your time is limited because you have to catch a plane to go back to Houston for chemotherapy, and we appreciate you and your wife making the trip all the way to Washington, and wish you both a quick recovery.

Specialist Cody Full was a Specialist in Sergeant Bergdahl's squad at the time he disappeared, and they were previously roommates together.

Mr. Mike Waltz is the Senior National Security Fellow at the New America Foundation. Mr. Waltz commanded a Special Forces Company in eastern Afghanistan at the time Sergeant Bergdahl was captured. He was previously a Senior Defense Department Coordinator for Afghanistan and Vice President Cheney's Counterterrorism Advisor.

And then Dr. Mark Davidson is the Senior Advisor at the Truman National Security Project, Adjunct Professor at George Washington University. He previously advised both General Stanley McChrystal and General David Petraeus, and has served on the staff of the Senate Armed Services Committee.

We will start with Mr. Andrews. You have 5 minutes, sir. You will need to turn on the microphone. It's that little button in front of you.

STATEMENT OF MR. ANDY ANDREWS, FATHER OF DECEASED SECOND LIEUTENANT, USA, DARRYN ANDREWS

Mr. ANDREWS. Thank you, Mr. Chairman, ranking members and members of the subcommittee. I am Andy Andrews, father of Second Lieutenant Darryn Deen Andrews who was killed in Afghanistan during the process for searching for Bowe Bergdahl.

Darryn's first tour in Afghanistan was in 2004 as an enlisted soldier. He developed a medical condition that required surgery so he was sent to Germany, and then back to the States. He applied to the Green to Gold program and was accepted into it. He enrolled in 2006 at Texas State University in San Marcos, Texas to complete his Master's degree while enrolled in ROTC.

He was commissioned to Second Lieutenant of the U.S. Army. He was stationed at Fort Benning, Georgia, then briefly at Fort Richardson, Alaska before being sent to Afghanistan in April 2009.

We were able to talk to Darryn by telephone whenever he got the chance to call. We conversed with him around July 1st or 3rd. His birthday is on the 3rd. He told us they had been out looking for the last 24 hours for this soldier who had walked away. I asked if the soldier had been captured while on guard duty. Darryn said he didn't think so because all of his gear was found neatly stacked, so he thought the soldier had just left. The soldier's name was not mentioned, so all we knew was that a soldier had left.

Darryn could not tell us where he was, or what they were doing. When we would talk to him in the next few months, we would occasionally ask if they had found the soldier, and he would say no, they were still looking. No name or specifics were ever mentioned.

Darryn was killed on September 4th, 2009 which coincidentally, was our 41st wedding anniversary. Second Lieutenant Darryn Deen Andrews distinguished himself by extraordinary heroism in combat as the Platoon Leader of the 3rd Platoon Blackfoot Company, First Battalion, 501st Infantry Airborne in support of Operation Enduring Freedom. Darryn's wife and son, his twin brother Jarrett and his family were in Cameron, Texas to celebrate Daylan's, which is Darryn's son, second birthday on September 7th. My wife and I had been on the coast to celebrate our anniversary. We had just pulled into our driveway and started to unload the truck. Jarrett had come over and told us that Darryn's wife's neighbor had called to tell her that the Army was looking for her. This was approximately 15:30 hours. We told him that we would call her and tell her to be back at the house at 18:30 hours. I unhooked the boat, and we all went to New Braunfels.

The Army notification team arrived at approximately 19:00 hours. The Sergeant told us that Darryn had been killed on September 4th, and he would probably still be alive if he had remained in the truck like most officers would have instead of getting out of the truck to help get it out of the hole the IED had made. We were told he had saved soldiers lives when he spotted enemy combatant fire, an RPG, shoved others out of the way and alerted other soldiers. Darryn took a direct hit from the RPG.

When we attended a memorial service for Darryn and other soldiers killed in Afghanistan, Lieutenant Colonel Baker's wife hosted a luncheon for us. At that luncheon, Captain Silvino Silvino Sandoval told us exactly how Darryn was killed. He stated they were on a mission to locate high interest Taliban and were passing through a village. The road had walls on each side and room to maneuver was limited. The lead vehicle hit an IED and was disabled, because of the walls were on each side around the vehicle was not possible. They got out to assess the damage. Darryn had Staff Sergeant Zavodny and PFC Martinec with him. Darryn saw the enemy combatant step from behind the wall and fire an RPG. Darryn yelled RPG and pushed Zavodny and Martinec to the ground, and then Darryn took a direct hit from the RPG. Staff Sergeant Zavodny received some damage to his ears, and Private Martinec survived the airlift to Germany, but died a few days later.

On February 12th, 2010, Second Lieutenant Darryn Deen Andrews was posthumously awarded the Silver Star for his heroic actions. At no time during this was it mentioned that he was searching for Bergdahl, only searching for a high interest Taliban.

When Bergdahl was portrayed on television as serving with honor and distinction by State by Susan Rice. The soldiers who were there contacted my wife to make sure we knew, we understood what a hero was, and was not, and Bergdahl's walking away was a contributing factor in Darryn's death.

I saw the Lieutenant Colonel on the television state, ''If you want to know what happened ask the enlisted people, don't ask the officers because the enlisted people can tell you exactly what happened.'' We received testimony from six different soldiers, the same testimony that Bergdahl walked away and was not captured, and that Darryn was killed while searching for him. Thank you.

[The prepared statement of Mr. Andrews follows:]

Written Testimony: Andy Andrews

Thank you Mr. Chairman, ranking members and members of the sub committees.

I am Andy Andrews, Father of 2LT Darryn Deen Andrews who was killed in Afghanistan while in the process of searching for Bowe Bergdahl.

Darryn's first tour in Afghanistan was in 2004 as an enlisted soldier. He developed a medical condition that required surgery so he was sent to Germany and then back to the states. He applied to the Green to Gold program and was accepted into it. He enrolled in 2006 at Texas State University in San Marcos, Texas to complete his Master's degree while enrolled in ROTC. He was commissioned a second lieutenant in the U.S. Army. He was stationed at Ft. Benning, GA then briefly at Ft. Richardson, AK before being sent to Afghanistan in April of 2009. We were able to talk to Darryn by telephone whenever he got a chance to call. We conversed with him around July 1 or 2. His birthday is on the third. He told us they had been out looking for the last 24 hours for this soldier who had walked away. I asked if the soldier had been captured while on guard duty. Darryn said he didn't think so because all his gear was found neatly stacked so he thought the soldier had just left. The soldier's name was not mentioned so all we knew was that a soldier had left. Darryn could not tell us where he was or what they were doing. When we would talk to him the next few months we would occasionally ask if they had found their soldier and he would say they had not and were still looking. No name or specifics were ever mentioned.

Darryn was killed on September 4, 2009 which coincidentally was our 41st wedding anniversary. 2LT Darryn Deen Andrews distinguished himself by extraordinary heroism in combat as the platoon leader for 3rd Platoon, Blackfoot Company, 1st Battalion, 501st Infantry (Airborne) in support of OPERATION ENDURING FREEDOM.

Darryn's wife and son, his twin brother, Jarrett, and his family were in Cameron, Texas to celebrate Daylan's (Darryn's son) second birthday on the September 7th. My wife and I had been on the coast to celebrate our anniversary. We had just pulled into our driveway and started to unload the truck. Jarrett came over and told us that Darryn's wife's neighbor had called to tell her that the army was looking for her. This was approximately 1530 hours. He told them that he would call her and tell her to be back at the house at 1830 hours. I unhooked the boat and we all went to New Braunfels. The Army notification team arrived at approximately 1900 hours. The sergeant told us that Darryn had been killed on Sept 4th and he would probably still be alive if he had remained in the truck like most officers would have instead of getting out of the truck to help get it out of the hole the IED had made. We were told he had saved soldiers' lives when he spotted an enemy combatant fire a RPG, shoved others out of the way and alerted other soldiers. Darryn took a direct hit from the RPG.

We attended a memorial service for Darryn and the soldiers of the 501st killed on this deployment on or about September 13. During the days in Anchorage Darryn's commanding officer Lt. Colonel Baker's wife hosted a luncheon for us. At the luncheon Darryn's captain, Capt. Silvino Silvino Sandoval told us exactly how Darryn was killed. He stated that they were on a mission to locate a high interest Taliban and were passing through a village. The road had walls on each side and room to maneuver was limited. The lead vehicle hit an IED and was disabled. Because of the walls on each side of the road going around the vehicle was not possible. Soldiers got out to assess damage and get the vehicle out of the hole. Darryn had SSG Zavodny and PFC Martinec with him. Darryn saw the enemy combatant step from behind a wall and fire a RPG. Darryn yelled "RPG!!!" and pushed Zavodny and Martinec to the ground. Darryn took a direct hit from the RPG. SSG Zavodny received some damage to his ears. PFC Martinec survived to be airlifted to Germany but died a few days later. Lt. Andrews' warning gave his men time to seek cover preventing more severe injuries and loss of life. At no time was it mentioned they were engaged is searching for private Bergdahl during this mission or any other mission.

On February 12, 2010 2LT Darryn Deen Andrews was posthumously awarded the Silver Star for his heroic actions. During this ceremony the Cameron Independent School District renamed the Cameron Elementary/Junior High library the "2LT Darryn Deen Andrews Memorial Library". The narrative of the Silver Star documentation states that Lt Darryn Andrews was killed as Captain Silvino described. At no point in the document is the search for Pvt. Bergdahl mentioned.

When Bergdahl was portrayed on television as having served with honor and distinction as stated by Susan Rice the soldiers who were there contacted my wife to make sure she knew they understood what a hero was and what was not and Bergdahl's walking away was a contributing factor in Darryn's death. Darryn and Bowe Bergdahl were not in the same platoon. Bergdahl was in the second platoon and Darryn was the leader of the third platoon. The soldiers told us that everybody was searching for Bergdahl. Six soldiers who were serving with Darryn at the time of his death have confirmed with my wife and me that when Darryn was killed while on a mission to find Bergdahl. A member of Army intelligence who was there at the same time Darryn was came to our house last week and told us everyone based in the vicinity was instructed to search for Bergdahl every time they went out. He related to us that he was supposed to go to another post to question locals but could not get transportation because all available helicopters were tied up searching for Bergdahl. He stated that Bergdahl's desertion disrupted the mission of the entire unit. Lt. Colonel Baker, Darryn's commander, called last week. He reiterated that the only mission Darryn was on was to search for the high ranking Taliban and the soldiers with Darryn probably did not have the security clearance to know what the mission was.

I do know that the men who were there believe he was a factor. They also believe he is a deserter. The enemy knew we were looking for him and they knew how to most effectively attack us. Did Bergdahl desert? I think so from what our son and soldiers who were there told my wife and me. There most definitely needs to be a through, non-political investigation in his leaving and the five years he was missing. I heard a Lt. Colonel on TV state that if one wants to know what is going on in the military do not ask the colonels or generals. Ask the lower ranks. They can tell you what really happened. My information was obtained from the enlisted soldiers who were there with my son and I believe it to be credible information.

Since Bergdahl was released we have been interviewed by many news media in the United States and Britain. We participate in these interviews because we want our son remembered for his heroic actions so someday his children can read about him with pride. His son turned two three days after he was killed and his daughter was born about three and one-half months after he was killed. The only thing they will know about him is his story.

R.G. 'Andy" Andrews

Father of 2LT Darryn Deen Andrews

Mr. Poe. Thank you, Mr. Andrews. The committee now will hear from Specialist Full.

STATEMENT OF SPC. CODY FULL, USA, RETIRED (SERVED WITH SGT. BERGDAHL IN BLACKFOOT COMPANY, SECOND PLATOON)

Mr. Full. Chairman, ranking members and members of the subcommittee, thank you for allowing me to share my firsthand account of my experiences serving in Afghanistan.

One of the first things I noticed about Bergdahl when he arrived in our unit, he was always asking questions. He seemed focused, he was well read, intelligent, blended in as he needed to be, always at the right place, right time, right uniform.

In November I got deployed to the National Training Center to train for an upcoming deployment to Afghanistan. During this time, myself, or anybody I've spoken with can't remember Bergdahl walking off the base and abandoning his team. This story seems to be repeated over and over again. I have no idea why. We would have at least heard about that or known it was happening. It did not happen.

In March 2009, our brigade deployed to Afghanistan but Bergdahl did not make the deployment with us. He had gotten a staph infection and would not make it until May 2009.

Soon after arriving in Afghanistan, we were tasked with building an overview called Observation Post MEST. While there we were on the front lines digging holes for bunkers, filling sandbags, driving T posts, hanging wire, all grilling tasks in themselves in 100 degree weather, go ahead and add your equipment, it's very tough. We were told we could take some items of clothing off to keep us from having a heat stroke. Security was always set in place. Nobody was ever in jeopardy. This has been used against us saying that we were a band of outlaws or misfits, not the case. Leaders were reprimanded for that by somebody higher up. We in the platoon felt that it was without merit.

After arriving in Afghanistan, it didn't take long for Bergdahl to start voicing his disagreements with the way our missions were being led. He didn't understand why we were doing more humanitarian missions instead of hunting the Taliban. Our Team Leader and Squad Leader both told Bergdahl that those were our orders and we will follow them.

Before we went out to OP MEST the day of June 30, 2009, about a week before we were told this is the last time we would ever go out to this observation post. During this time, Bergdahl mailed his items home or to a family friend. He mailed them back to the States. We didn't know this until after we got back, after he deserted, and we found that his equipment had been mailed home.

On the night of June 30th, excuse me, the morning of June 30th, 100 percent accountability was held around 6 a.m. Everyone was given the proper number of men and equipment except for 3rd Squad Alpha Team, which was my team, the squad that Bergdahl was in. Platoon members immediately started searching the tiny observation post for missing items. We looked under cots, the latrine, under trucks, everywhere we could think. Bergdahl was nowhere to be found. In a single man tent Bergdahl been sleeping in we found his gun, ammo and plate carrier.

Patrols were immediately kicked out to the surrounding area to look for Bergdahl. According to some small children we spoke to they had seen a single American matching Bergdahl's description crawling low on the ground through the reeds earlier that day on their way to school. The story was also confirmed by a cleric and a teacher that saw the same thing.

A few days later we heard from our interpreter that the American that was walking around in the Afghan village looking for somebody that spoke English and water also wanted to seek out the Taliban. That was from the interpreter speaking it directly to us.

After Bergdahl was found that he walked off, DUSTWAN was called up that his duty status and whereabouts unknown. Every asset in Afghanistan was pushed to this effort. After Bergdahl shipping his items home, local accounts of seeing him crawling and asking for the Taliban, the false stories he emailed his father and odd questions all helped us connect the dots later, but at the time of the unfolding of the events it seemed like normal off-the-wall jargon common when the infantry is deployed.

The facts tell me that Bergdahl's desertion was premeditated. He had a plan and was trying to justify it in his head. How long he had planned this I do not know, but it is clear to me that he had a plan and executed it. Countless people looked for him when he went missing putting their own lives on the line for his.

Combat is difficult. The only thing you can count on in combat is the commitment of your fellow Americans. Knowing that someone you needed to trust deserted you in war and did so of his own free will is the ultimate betrayal.

Now that Bergdahl is back in the United States an investigation needs to take place as to why he left us. All the documents, including the intelligence known on Bergdahl now need to come to the public view. Americans need to also see the original investigation on Bergdahl's desertion. You should not be able to desert your fellow Americans without consequences. Bowe Bergdahl should not be characterized as having served with honor and distinction. Any armed service member who violates UCMJ is punished. Bergdahl should not be an exception. If Bergdahl hadn't deserted us, he would never been held in captivity.

In my opinion, Bowe Bergdahl needs to be charged with desertion, missing movement, disrespect for a superior commissioned officer, insubordinate conduct toward non-commissioned officer, failure to obey order or regulation, misbehavior before the enemy, and misconduct as prisoner. Thank you.

[The prepared statement of Mr. Full follows:]

Cody Herbert Full

Honorably Discharged 11/11/11 from US ARMY

Served in 3rd squad 2nd Platoon Blackfoot Company, 1-501 PIR 4/25 BCT

Jan 08-Nov 11

House Committee on Foreign Affairs

June 18, 2014

Chairman Royce, Members of the Foreign Affairs committee, thank you for allowing me to share my first-hand account of my experiences serving in Afghanistan.

I arrived at FT. Richardson at the end of January 2008; I was assigned to Blackfoot company 2nd platoon. 1-501 Battalion, 4th Brigade 25th Infantry Division. Bowe Bergdahl arrived to 2nd PLT around Oct 2008. I want to share some of my observances about Bowe Bergdahl, since I was around him a lot. In fact, he was my roommate.

One of the first things I noticed about Bergdahl was that he was always asking questions and taking notes. He seemed focused. Bergdahl was well-read, intelligent and blended in as well as he needed to. Upon arriving, though, Bergdahl made comments about how he wanted to kill as many Taliban as he could. I never heard him say anything about helping the Afghan people; his comments were all about killing as many Taliban as he could.

In November 2008 our unit deployed to the National Training Center in California to train for our upcoming deployment to Afghanistan. During this time Bergadahl was a good solider; he was on time, in the right uniform, taking notes and asking questions. During this time neither I nor anybody I have spoken with and served with can remember Bergdahl walking off the base and abandoning his team. While this story seems to be repeated over and over, I don't believe it happened. Platoon members would have known if someone walked off or noticed if someone wasn't in their proper place. We would at least heard about it and no one there can remember it happening.

I've recently heard another story that doesn't make sense. Bergdahl's father has referred to an email, reported by a magazine, that his son became friends with a LT Bradshaw while at NTC. Bradshaw was part of Comanche Company. Officers from other companies do not fraternize with the lower enlisted. Comanche Company was not even in the same area as our Blackfoot company while at NTC.

The only time Bergadahl could have spoken to LT Bradshaw was in passing. The idea that Bergdahl and Bradshaw were close friends or even friends is false in every sense; this has been vetted by common knowledge of how an infantry brigade structure works as well as speaking with former members of Bradshaw's PLT and friends of LT Bradshaw.

In March of 2009 our Brigade deployed to Afghanistan but Bergdahl did not make the deployment with us. He had gotten a staph infection and would not make it until May 2009.

Soon after arriving in Afghanistan, we were tasked with building an observation post called OP MEST, named for the location of the post. While at OP MEST, platoon members including Bergadahl were photographed out of uniform and in short sleeves. This is a common occurrence for military members on the front lines. After all, it's hot and dirty and tough work. This photograph has been used by some to say our platoon had problems. It's a ridiculous charge. Security was always in place. These acts of common sense survival did not jeopardize the security or put anyone in danger. Leaders in the platoon, however, were reprimanded and punished after the photos were released to the media. Many of us didn't agree with the punishment and felt it was without merit. At the same time, we received a new leader called a PL (Lieutenant). Morale was restored and even raised with the leader because we finally had a PL who inspired and actually led from the front. The reports about our PLT having discipline problems have been taken out of context told in half-truths and are simply false.

It didn't take long for Bergdahl to start voicing his disagreements with the way our missions were being led. He didn't understand why we were doing more humanitarian aid drops, setting up clinics, and helping the populous instead of hunting the Taliban. At one point, Bergdahl said, "Why can't we dress like the locals and ambush the Taliban". In my opinion Bergdahl wanted to do the exact opposite of what we were instructed to do. He wanted to hunt and kill. He was clearly frustrated that we were instructed to win the hearts and minds of the local populous. Bergdahl was told by our Team

Leader and Squad leader, these are our orders and we will follow them. But Bergdahl was not happy about not getting to shoot and kill.

A week or two prior to Bergdahl deserting our platoon, we were tasked to help a QRF (Quick Reaction Force) that had struck an IED in the mountains near Omna. They needed assistance and aid and our PLT was tasked to quickly help; it took around 8 hours to get to the other team. While making our way up the switchbacks, a truck in the middle of the convoy struck an IED. Another truck towed the blown up truck to the Afghan National Army/Afghan National Police's Omna compound. Security was set in place and our platoon remained there for 6 days waiting for the truck parts, with supplies for us like water, fuel, ammo and food airdropped in. While there waiting, Bergdahl told us "I could see myself getting lost in these mountains". It was an odd thing to say since we were alone in a combat zone.

Once set, our PLT took a different route leaving and an ambush soon took place. It started with an IED in middle of the convoy and continued with RPGs, Machine gun fire and AKs. Our PLT was surrounded by the enemy with the enemy having high ground, cover and concealment. It was a tense situation and one that Bergdahl had claimed he was itching for. Bergdahl was in the lead truck but in the back as a passenger holding his machine gun when the truck's main gun went down. The guys up front urgently needed a backup gun from one of the two SAW gunners in the back seat where Bergdahl was. A machine gun was passed up along with ammo to the truck's gunner. What's troubling for me is that a version of this story has been told to the media portraying Bergdahl as frustrated with his superiors and platoon members because he didn't get to fight. Yet he claimed to want to walk into the mountains alone.

Another war story that Bergdahl told in an **email to his father stated**:

"We don't even care when we hear each talk about running children down in the dirt streets with our armored trucks…" This is completely false. Our unit did NOT run over a child. In fact, we didn't run over anyone at all.

Other emails Bergdahl sent his father stated "…I am ashamed to even be American…the horror that America is disgusting…There are a few more boxes coming to you guys, feel free to open them and use them."

This tells us a few things, what Bergdahl was telling his platoon members and what he was telling his parents were polar opposites. In reality, we were doing exactly what Bergdahl was telling his parents we should be doing. For some reason, he was complaining to his parents about events that weren't happening; and complaining to us about what we were actually doing. Bergdahl said in emails he wanted us to help the afghan people, but in real life he disagreed with this and wanted to kill more. Bergdahl was complaining to his parents that our PLT was committing atrocities instead of helping the local populous but he was telling our PLT that we needed to stop trying to win hearts and minds and focus more on killing the Taliban.

About a week before June 30th 2009, our PLT was told this would be the last time we would be going out to OP MEST. We would be tasked to a different area, one more 5 day rotation and we would be done. It was during this time that Bergdahl sent his personal items home. We did not know this at the time but only found out after he deserted us. While returning to FOB Sharana, members of the PLT were tasked with inventorying Bergdhal's equipment and property. His missing items were discovered then.

While out at OP MEST for the last time, Bergdahl asked one platoon member "If your M9 (9mm Beretta Pistol) went missing, would you get into trouble?" The platoon member responded with "yes".

On June 29th we were told that we would be leaving OP MEST a day earlier than scheduled so June 30th 2009 would be our last night.

On June 30th 2009, 100% accountability was around 6 am local time. 100% is done every morning and every night, leaders check all sensitive equipment like Night vision, Gun, Optics and anything that has a serial number and could aid enemy if lost. Everyone was good on the proper number of men and equipment except 3rd squad Alpha Team, my team and Squad. PLT members immediately started searching the tiny OP for the missing items. We looked under cots, the latrine, in trucks, under trucks, in different trucks, everywhere we could think to look. Bowe Bergdahl was nowhere to be found. In the single man tent Bergdahl had been sleeping in we found his gun, ammo and plate carrier.

Patrols were immediately kicked out in the surrounding areas to look for Bergdahl. According to some school children we spoke to, they had seen a single American matching Bergdahl's description crawling low on the ground through the reeds earlier in the day on their way to school. This story was also confirmed by a Cleric and a Teacher who saw the same thing. A couple of days later we heard over the radio via our interpreter that there was an American looking for someone in the Afghan village who spoke English. The witness said he needed some water and wanted to talk to the Taliban. During this time or very shortly after DUSTWAN was called up on the radio. The process of trying to find him before calling up DUSTWAN happened for many reasons. DUSTWAN is sort of like BROKENARROW once it's called up all assets are pushed to that effort; you want to make damn sure that he indeed needs DUSTWAN before calling it up.

Bergdahl shipping his items home, local accounts of seeing him crawling and asking for the Taliban, the false stories he emailed to his father and the odd questions he was asking all helped us to connect the dots later. But at the time of the unfolding events, it seemed like normal off the wall BS common with the infantry when deployed. The facts tell me that Bergdahl's desertion was pre-mediated. Bergdahl had a plan and was trying to justify it in his head. How long he had planned this I don't know, but it is clear to me that he had a plan and executed it. Countless people looked for him when he went missing, putting their own lives on the line for his. I have said it before and I will say again here, I do not know how he felt about us in the platoon but we all would have died for him.

Combat is difficult. The only thing you can count on in combat is the commitment of your fellow American. Knowing that someone you needed to trust deserted you in war and did it by his own free will is the ultimate betrayal.

Now that Bergdahl is back in the United States, an investigation needs to take place as to why he left us. All of the documents, including the intelligence, known on Bergdahl now need to come to the public view. Americans need to also see the original investigation on Bergdahl's desertion. You should not be able to desert your fellow Americans without consequences. Bowe Bergdahl should not be characterized as having served with Honor and Distinction. Any armed service member who violates UCMJ gets punished; Bergdahl should not be an exception. If Bergdahl hadn't deserted us then he would have never been held in captivity.

In my opinion, Bowe Bergdahl needs to be charged with the following:

Article 85-Desertion: (1) without authority goes or remains absent from his unit, organization or place of duty with intent to remain away there from permanently (2) quits his unit, organization or place of duty with intent to avoid hazardous duty or to shrink important service

Article 87- Missing Movement: Any person subject to this chapter who through neglect or design misses the movement if a ship, aircraft or unit with which he is required in the course of duty

Article 89-Disrepect toward superior commissioned officer: Any person subject to this chapter who behaves with disrespect towards his superior commissioned officer

Article 90- Willfully disobeying his superior officer: (2) willfully disobeys a lawful command of his superior commissioned officer

Article 91- Insubordinate conduct toward Non-Commissioned Officer: (2) willfully disobeys the lawful order of an NCO

Article 92- Failure to Obey Order or Regulation: (1) violates or fails to obey any lawful general order (2) having knowledge of any other lawful order issued by any member of the armed forces, which it his duty to obey the order (3) is derelict in the performance of his duties

Article 99- Misbehavior before the enemy- (1) runs away (2) shamefully abandons, surrenders, or delivers up any command, unit, place or military property which it is his duty to defend (3) through disobedience, neglect or intentional misconduct endangers the safety of any such command, unit, place or military property (4) cast away his arms or ammunition (5) is guilty of cowardly conduct

Article 105- Misconduct as Prisoner: (1) for purpose of securing favorable treatment by his captors acts without proper authority in manner contrary to law, custom or regulation to the detriment of others of whatever nationality held by the enemy as civilian or military prisoners.

Thank you.

Mr. POE. Thank you, Mr. Full. Mr. Waltz, your testimony for 5 minutes, please.

STATEMENT OF MR. MIKE WALTZ, SENIOR NATIONAL SECURITY FELLOW, NEW AMERICA FOUNDATION (COMMANDED A SPECIAL FORCES' COMPANY IN EASTERN AFGHANISTAN IN 2009)

Mr. WALTZ. Mr. Chairman, Madam Chairman, ranking members, thank you for holding this hearing today on a subject of vital national importance.

I, too, want to take just a moment to pay tribute to the family members of the thousands who served their country in this conflict, particularly the Andrews family that are here with us today. At the end of the day, we volunteered, we volunteered to go but the families have to deal with the consequences of our service.

On June 30th, 2009, I commanded a U.S. Army Special Forces Company with responsibility for operations in Afghanistan, particularly Paktika Province where then Private Bergdahl went missing. That evening two of my special forces teams boarded helicopters on a mission to search an Afghan compound where we had indication that Bergdahl may be held. This marked the beginning of several weeks worth of missions into some of the most hostile areas of Afghanistan and the Pakistan border to find him.

Within days we received orders to halt all other ongoing missions and initiatives; notably, including preparations for the 2009 Afghan National Elections. We were ordered to devote all resources and energy to the search for Bergdahl. It soon became apparent, however, that the Taliban knew we were conducting an all-out search for him and they began feeding false information to our informant network in order to lure our forces into a trap.

On several occasions, my men were lured into ambushes, including an Afghan home rigged with explosives, a car bomb that was primed to explode, and other types of deadly traps. Fortunately, the bombs failed to explode in those situations, but they were too close for comfort. Other soldiers, as we know, were not so fortunate.

All of us commonly understood at the time that Bergdahl had walked off his post after a guard shift into a local Afghan village. We knew, though, that we had to do whatever it took to find him, and that was fine. But I have to tell you, all of my men, me included, were absolutely furious and resentful, frankly, that a fellow American soldier had put us into this position. It violated the most fundamental and basic ethos of being a soldier and a soldier's creed.

I'll leave further speculation regarding his state of mind of his motives to my fellow witnesses who knew him personally, but I am confident in saying Sergeant Bergdahl endangered the lives of thousands of men and women sent to search for him. He diverted scarce and valuable resources such as predator drones, helicopters, IED clearing teams from other units that desperately needed those assets.

Wittingly or unwittingly, he handed our enemies a significant propaganda tool that they repeatedly used in videos to denounce the United States and recruit for their cause.

And, finally, we all know that he handed the Taliban's leadership a strategic bargaining tool that they effectively used to free five of their most senior leaders, what I call the Taliban war cabinet.

I just want to take a moment, I think it's important to put the release of these men in the broader context of our policy toward Afghanistan. As I'm sure you are aware, millions of Afghans voted in the runoff election this past Saturday. They are in the midst of one of the most sensitive and unprecedented political transitions in their history. In my view, there are still significant questions whether they will succeed.

Every Afghan that I've spoken to from civilian society, to government officials are stunned that we would release these individuals back into their society. We have to keep in mind, these men were household names, particularly they're household names of the worst kind, particularly the women and minorities that were slaughtered at their hands.

It's the timing, though, of this release that has some of these groups particularly perplexed. We spent the last year dueling and cajoling President Karzai to sign a long-term security agreement with us, the Bilateral Security Agreement. Both of the final candidates to replace Karzai have indicated they would sign it, yet weeks before the Presidential election, the administration announces a full withdrawal of all U.S. forces by the end of '16, essentially a zero option, and then we have restocked the Taliban war cabinet. So, even if the Government of Qatar is able to prevent these men from returning to their own ways, what's going to happen a year from now? You know, a year in that part of the world is a blink of an eye to people who have long memories and a long view toward their objectives.

You know, one can understand the confusion and transparency, and trepidation, excuse me, of even the most ardent supporters of a strong Afghan-U.S. relationship, so where does that leave our policy going forward? In my view, it's one of hope and assumption. We're assuming the Afghan army can hold its ground, we're assuming there will be no ethnic violence as part of the transition. We're assuming reconciliation talks will resume in our favor. And, most importantly, we're assuming that al-Qaeda can't reconstitute like it has in Iraq and as in Syria.

And I would just leave you with a word of caution. If that scares us, and what's going on right now with ISIS, and Iraq, and Syria should, what's going to happen when we're dealing with a nuclear arsenal in Pakistan? I have other views, but I'm happy to answer a question on AUMF and on future GITMO release, but I am out of time, and with that I will stop, sir.

[The prepared statement of Mr. Waltz follows:]

The Bergdahl Exchange:
Implications for U.S. National Security and
the Fight Against Terrorism

Michael G. Waltz
Senior National Security Fellow
New America Foundation

Hearing before the
House Committee on Foreign Affairs
Subcommittee on Terrorism, Nonproliferation, and Trade

Washington, DC
June 18, 2014

Mr. Chairman, Madam Chairman, Ranking Member Sherman, Ranking Member Deutch, and Members of the Joint Subcommittee, thank you for holding this hearing today on a subject of vital national importance - the Implications of the exchange of Sgt. Bowe Bergdahl on the fight against terrorism.

I want to first take this opportunity to thank the many Americans, military and civilian, who have served our country in Afghanistan and Pakistan over the past decade since 9/11. Most importantly, I want to pay tribute to the family members of the hundreds of thousands who have served our country in this conflict, particularly the Andrews family that is with us here today.

On June 30, 2009, the day then-Private Bergdahl went missing, I commanded a U.S. Army Special Forces company with responsibility for operations in Ghazni, Khost, Paktia, and Paktika provinces where then Private Bergdahl when missing.[1] That evening two of my Special Forces teams boarded helicopters on a mission to search an Afghan compound where we had indication that Bergdahl may be held. This marked the beginning of several week's worth of missions into some of the most hostile areas of Afghanistan to find him. The basic strategy was to use conventional U.S. infantry units along with the Afghan Army and police to man a series of checkpoints round the clock on key roads and mountain passes in an effort to prevent the Taliban from escaping with Bergdahl across the border into Pakistan's tribal areas. Simultaneously, my Special Forces teams and other special operations units conducted raids into locations suspected of harboring Bergdahl or his captors.   Within days we received orders to halt all other ongoing missions and initiatives – notably, including preparations to secure the Afghan National Elections to be held that fall – in order to devote all energy and resources to the search for Bergdahl. It soon became

---

[1] The opinions and analyses expressed in this testimony are solely those of the author. The description of the author as "former commander of Army Special Forces in Afghanistan" is for identification purposes only and does not imply in any way approval by the Department of Defense or the United States Government of the views herein expressed.

apparent that the Taliban knew we were conducting an all-out search for him and they began feeding false information into our network of informants in order to lure our forces into a trap. On several occasions, particularly in Ghazni Province, my men were lured into ambushes, including an Afghan home rigged with explosives, and a car bomb primed to explode. Fortunately, the bombs failed to detonate but those situations were far too close for comfort. Other soldiers were not so fortunate and gave their lives on missions directly or indirectly dedicated to the search. All of us commonly understood at the time that Bergdahl had walked off his post after a guard shift into a local Afghan village where he was apprehended by members of the Haqqani network. We knew we had to do whatever we could to get him back but all of my men, me included, were absolutely furious and resentful frankly that a fellow American soldier had put us in this position. It violated the most fundamental and basic ethos of a soldier's creed – to never put the men and women to the left and right of you in harm's way. I'll leave speculation regarding his motives or state of mind that night to my fellow witnesses who knew him personally in addition to the ongoing Army investigation.

I am confident in saying that Sgt. Bergdahl endangered the lives of the thousands of men and women sent to search for him. He diverted scarce and valuable resources such a Predator drones, helicopters, and IED clearing teams from other missions and units that desperately needed them. Finally, wittingly or unwittingly, he handed our enemies, the Taliban and the Haqqani Network, a significant propaganda tool that they repeatedly used in videos to denounce the United States and recruit for their cause. Ultimately, Sgt. Bergdahl's actions provided the Taliban's leadership with a strategic bargaining tool that they effectively used to free five of their most senior leaders, what I call the Taliban War Cabinet. Let's take a moment and examine the price we paid in this exchange:

By way of background, the Taliban has long sought the release of these five men, all of whom are experienced jihadists and helped run the

Taliban's operations in pre-9/11 Afghanistan. Several were also critical to the Taliban's external relations with al Qaeda, Iran, and other regional extremist groups. They served in various military and intelligence roles. All five of the detainees were deemed "high" risks to the U.S. and its allies by Joint Task Force Guantanamo (JTF-GTMO) and were judged as highly likely to return to extremist activities. Two of the five are reportedly wanted by the UN for war crimes.

Abdul Haq Wasiq: a former Taliban intelligence official, Wasiq had direct access to Taliban and Hezb-e-Islami Gulbuddin (HIG) leadership, according to open source reporting on JTF-GTMO threat assessments. Wasiq was central to the Taliban's efforts to form alliances with other Islamic fundamentalist groups to fight alongside the Taliban against U.S. and Coalition forces after 9/11. JTF-GTMO concluded that Wasiq utilized his office to support al Qaeda and to assist Taliban personnel to elude capture in late 2001. Wasiq also arranged for al Qaeda personnel to train Taliban staff in intelligence gathering methods.

Mullah Norullah Noori: a Taliban military commander, reportedly fought alongside Taliban and al Qaeda since the 1990s. Noori was instrumental in hosting al Qaeda in Afghanistan and facilitating their support. He apparently served as an intermediary between Osama Bin Laden and Mullah Omar. His brother is reportedly still an active senior leader within the Taliban and he is wanted by the United Nations (UN) for possible war crimes including the murder of thousands of Shiite Muslims.

Mullah Mohammad Fazl: a Taliban deputy minister of defense, and one of the Taliban's most experienced commanders prior to his capture in November 2001. Like Noori, according to JTF-GTMO files now available online, Fazl is wanted by the UN for possible war crimes including the murder of thousands of Shiites. Fazl worked closely with Bin Laden's Arab 055 Brigade that actively fought the ethnic Tajik's in Ahmed Shah Massood's Northern Alliance during the Taliban rule. Photographs are currently circulating the internet showing Fazl posing

33

with a knife behind the heads of a half dozen men.

Mullah Khairullah Khairkhwa: the former Taliban governor of Herat province in Western Afghanistan where he apparently liaised with Iranian officials on behalf of Mullah Omar. In June 2011, a DC district court denied Khairkhwa's petition for a writ of habeas corpus, based in large part on his admitted role in brokering the Taliban's post-9/11 relationship with the Iranian government.

Mohammad Nabi Omari: a senior Taliban leader that has served in a variety of leadership roles. Omari maintained very close ties to senior Haqqani network leadership and served as a coordinator and facilitator between al Qaeda, Taliban, and Haqqani operations.[2]

One has to wonder why, of all the terrorists still held in Guantanamo, the Taliban chose these five – essentially their top five draft picks.

It's important to put the release of these men in the broader context of our policy towards Afghanistan. As I'm sure you are aware, millions of Afghans voted in a runoff election this past Saturday the 14th of June. Afghanistan is currently in the midst of a sensitive and unprecedented political transition. In my view, there are still significant questions as to whether Afghanistan will enjoy its first peaceful political hand off of power in its long and violent history. Every Afghan I have spoken with in the past weeks, from civil society to government officials, are stunned that we would release these individuals back into their society. We must keep in mind that these men are household names of the worst kind in Afghanistan – particularly amongst women and the ethnic minorities that were slaughtered at their hands.

But, the timing of the release is what has these groups particularly

[2] Joscelyn, Thomas. "Sgt. Bowe Bergdahl Exchanged for Top 5 Taliban Commanders at Gitmo." The Long War Journal: A Project of the Foundation for Defense of Democracies. N.p., 31 May 2014. Web.

perplexed. We have spent the past year cajoling and dueling with President Karzai to sign a long term strategic agreement with the United States, the Bilateral Security Agreement. Both of the final candidates to replace Karzai have said they would sign the Agreement, yet, weeks before the presidential election in Afghanistan, the Obama Administration announced a full withdrawal of U.S. troops, by end of 2016. He then essentially re-stocked the Taliban War Cabinet with the release of the five Guantanamo detainees. Even if, the government of Qatar is able to prevent these men from returning to their old ways, what happens to them after the one year term on our agreement with the Qataris is over is an open ended question. One year is a blink of an eye in a part of the world with very long memories and that takes a very long term view towards obtaining their objectives. One can understand the confusion and trepidation even the most ardent Afghan supporters of their relationship with the United States are feeling right now.

Where does that leave our policy going forward? In my view, it's currently one of hope that is based on five critical assumptions:

1. We are assuming the Afghan National Army and police can stand on their own as we have predicted. My own experience on the ground over multiple tours as a Special Forces officer, leads me to believe our estimates are very optimistic. The problem is that we no longer have advisors at the operational level to know if the Army is failing. We may not know until it is too late.

2. We are assuming there will be a peaceful political transition this year. I think we run significant risks of severely escalated ethnic tensions regardless of who wins in the coming weeks. If the former foreign minister and presidential candidate Abdullah Abdullah wins we will have a Tajik-led government and a largely Tajik-led Afghan National Army against a Pashtun insurgency. If former finance minister Ghani wins I'm not sure Abdullah and his northern alliance supporters will

magnanimously swallow the bitter pill as they did when he lost to Karzai in 2009.

3. We are assuming that reconciliation talks will resume and end up with results aligned with our interests, even though we have practically given away all leverage by announcing the U.S. withdrawal years in advance.

4. We are hoping Afghanistan's neighbors – Russia, Iran, China, Pakistan, India – will not reignite old hatreds and strategic agendas in the wake of a U.S. withdrawal.

5. Most importantly, we are assuming that al Qaeda can't and won't stage a comeback in Pakistan and Afghanistan's lawless and inhospitable tribal border region as the coalition and the CIA withdraw their ability to pressure al Qaeda's leadership. We are grossly underestimating how dependent our intelligence agencies and civilian agencies are on our military presence in Afghanistan to be able to continue their work.

The implications of the trade of the five senior Taliban members are not just limited to Afghanistan, however. We must remind ourselves that the Taliban are part of syndicate of extremist groups spanning from West Africa across the Middle East and South Asia to the Philippines. They are just one regional jihadi insurgency amongst a constellation of groups. We must remember that al Qaeda's original goal was to overthrow apostate or un-Islamic regimes across the region and establish a caliphate in the Muslim world. Attacks on the West like 9/11 were just a tactical step to weaken our resolve in the region, lesson our support for Middle Eastern governments aligned with the West, and hopefully force withdrawals similar to Somalia in the 1990s. Whether it's the Taliban in Afghanistan, al Shabaab in Somalia, ISIS in the Levant, or other affiliated groups in Iraq, Yemen, and Uzbekistan, "a victory for one is a victory for all," as Secretary Gates once said in 2010. Sadly, Mullah Omar delivered a rare statement last week that declared the exchange for

Bergdahl a great victory for the Taliban movement.

All of those conflicts across Africa and the Middle East are very concerning. The events unfolding in Syria and Iraq right now are truly disturbing and cause for great concern. However, if one thinks that is bad, how frightening would it be if the keys to a nuclear arsenal were sitting in the capital of Iraq like they are in the capital of Pakistan? A destabilized Afghanistan could directly lead to a destabilized Pakistan along with its nuclear arsenal. The release of the Taliban's War Cabinet from Guantanamo in the midst of so much uncertainty in Afghanistan, upheaval across the Middle East, and terrorist organizations on the rise does not strike me as responsible or wise policy. It was a policy decision that was certainly not worth the sacrifices of the soldiers that gave everything to stabilize Afghanistan for future generations.

For these and other reasons, we need to take a close and careful look at future releases and the overall closure of Guantanamo. There has been much discussion of the relatively low recidivism rate of previously released detainees from Guantanamo. I would argue that quality matters much more than quantity here. Many of the previously released individuals were mid-level operatives that were deemed dangerous but an acceptable risk. Those detainees that are left are the cream of the crop of al Qaeda and their affiliates. I would also point out that Mullah Abdul Zakir, who was until recently the head of the Taliban military committee and Abu Bakr al-Baghdadi, the head of the Islamic State of Iraq and al Sham (ISIS) that is now terrorizing Iraq and Syria, were former detainees. I fully realize that the issue of Guantanamo is a difficult one, a problem that two administrations have grappled with, but we cannot become complacent about the intentions, capabilities, and near "rock-star" status that these men enjoy in extremist circles when they are released. We can't have it both ways. We can't argue to the world for over a decade that these men are too dangerous to bring on to American soil or to release, but then release them when it's expedient.

Finally, without straying too far from the reason I was requested to come here today, I would like to take this opportunity to urge both committees to think very carefully about calls to reform or even outright repeal the Authorization for Use of Military Force (AUMF) legislation. I am not a legal expert, but from my position as a special operator and a former policy advisor in the Pentagon and White House, I can say these authorities are critical to the successful prosecution of our war against extremism. We must not relegate this war back to a law enforcement problem. The law needs to be updated to be sure, but in light of what we are seeing from Libya to the Levant to Pakistan today we must not tie the hands of our military as they address these problems.

Thank you and I look forward to your questions.

38

Mr. POE. Thank you, Mr. Waltz. Dr. Jacobson, 5 minutes, please.

STATEMENT OF MARK JACOBSON, PH.D., SENIOR ADVISOR, TRUMAN NATIONAL SECURITY PROJECT

Mr. JACOBSON. Mr. Chairman, Madam Chairman, Ranking Members Sherman and Deutch, and distinguished members of the joint subcommittee, thank you for the opportunity to appear before you today.

I should first note that I, too, extend my gratitude to the Andrews family for the sacrifice they have made. I would like to have known their son. From what I have read and from what I have heard, he's a true hero.

I'm also honored to be sitting beside my friend, Mike Waltz, who is also a true patriot and a hero, and has served his nation bravely in Afghanistan. And thank you, Specialist Full, for your service, as well.

As someone who served in the Pentagon on September 11th, 2001, the threat posed by terrorism is not lost on me. While I had made the decision years before to devote myself to my nation, that day changed all of our lives forever. As a result, I spent several years in Afghanistan as a Naval Intelligence Officer, and later as a civilian advisor.

I am acutely aware of the danger that remains today in Afghanistan. For the four of us at the table, this conflict is personal and we all feel the impact of this war in a way most Americans do not.

One of the greatest commitments an American can make to their nation is to put on a uniform and take an oath to support and defend the Constitution of the United States. By taking this oath, these men and women make the selfless decision to put their country first. They do so knowing that they may be one day called to give that last full measure of devotion, to give their lives for their comrades, their families, and their nation. In exchange for that, the military makes its own promise, a promise to keep faith with those who have been captured. The commitment is simple, leave no man or woman behind, no exceptions. This commitment is unequivocal regardless of the circumstances of capture. This is something we owe to all those who have served, do serve, and will serve.

In short, this is why I believe that securing Sergeant Bergdahl's release was absolutely the right thing to do, and was worth the potential risks. Indeed, if Bergdahl did act improperly, then it is even more important that he brought home and held accountable in the military system for his actions.

While there is always risk when releasing detainees, those risks must be seen within a broader context. Indeed, the potential risks for the administration are no greater today than they were during the previous administration when 532 detainees were released from Guantanamo Bay. But there are reasons why given the situation today we should temper our concerns.

First, as outlined by Secretary of Defense Hagel, the Qatari government has committed to specific risk mitigation measures, including travel restrictions, monitoring, and other limitations. Second, there is not a consensus that these five individuals will inevitably return to the battlefield. And, if they do, the Afghanistan of 2014 is simply not the Afghanistan of 2001.

As Mike Waltz mentioned, the Afghan people have just gone through elections, 14 million ballots cast in two separate elections in open defiance of the Taliban. The strength of the insurgency will not regenerate because of the presence of five more individuals on the battlefield, especially since they've been off the battlefield for over a decade.

Some have questioned whether the recent prisoner exchange created new precedents that will endanger the lives of U.S. personnel. While the exchange of Sergeant Bergdahl took place before the end of the war in Afghanistan, in the past we have conducted prisoner exchanges before the end of hostilities, World War II and the Korean War, for example.

Likewise, the threat of kidnaping U.S. members of the armed forces by terrorists and insurgents has long been the case in Afghanistan. It was my own number one threat while I served in uniform. There is no reason to think that this calculus will be changed by the recent exchange.

Finally, the United States has been negotiating with the Taliban for some time now, a recognition that the war in Afghanistan cannot end without a political settlement. I understand the disappointment we feel in the stories coming out about Sergeant Bowe Bergdahl, and I understand the anger felt by some of his comrades who feel that he deliberately left his post. If I were them, I might feel the same way, but the truth is we do not yet know the whole truth.

In our nation of laws, the presumption of innocence is sacrosanct. People are innocent until proven guilty; thus, before passing judgment there must a thorough investigation. It must be allowed to take place without politics or partisanship. Without that we are unlikely to ever have accountability.

We may not like it, but in the end foreign affairs and national security policy are often about juggling bad options and finding the least worst approach. There are rarely simple solutions. The decision to exchange Sergeant Bergdahl may be imperfect, but it was the right decision. We never leave our soldiers behind.

Thank you again, Mr. Chairman, Madam Chairwoman, for inviting me to testify. I am pleased to stand ready for your questions.

[The prepared statement of Mr. Jacobson follows:]

June 17, 2014

Name: Mark R. Jacobson

Senior Advisor to the Truman National Security Project

House Committee on Foreign Affairs

June 18, 2014: "The Bergdahl Exchange: Implications for U.S. National Security and the Fight Against Terrorism"

Mr. Chairman, Madam Chairman, Ranking Member Sherman and Ranking Member Deutch and distinguished members of the Joint Subcommittee, thank you for the opportunity to appear before you to testify. Before I continue, I also wish to note that I am here as a Senior Advisor to the Truman National Security Project, and I am not here as a member of the Navy Reserve nor the Department of Defense, and my views do not represent those of either Department.

As someone who was in the Pentagon on September 11, 2001, the threat posed by terrorism is not lost on me. While I made the decision years before to devote myself to serving our nation, that day changed many of our lives forever. As a result I spent several years in Afghanistan – some as a Naval intelligence officer and some as a civilian advisor – and I am acutely aware of the danger that remains to Afghanistan. For all of us at the table the conflict in Afghanistan is personal and we all feel the impact of this war in a way most Americans do not.

I have been asked to address several issues pertinent to the Joint Committee's national security oversight responsibilities related to the potential risks incurred by exchanging SGT Bowe Bergdahl for five Afghan detainees held at Guantanamo Bay, Cuba and the potential precedent set by negotiating with terrorists or insurgents. In short, I believe that securing SGT Bergdahl's release was absolutely the right thing to do and was worth the potential risks.

One of the greatest commitments an American can make to their nation is to put on a uniform and take an oath as a member of the U.S. armed forces to "support and defend the Constitution of the United States." By taking this oath, these men and women – who are sons and daughters, fathers and mothers – make the selfless decision to put their country first. They do so knowing that they may one day be called to give what Abraham Lincoln called the "last full measure of devotion,"-- to give their lives for their comrades, their families, and their nation.

With each of these volunteers, the military makes its own promise to be there for those who have been captured. The commitment is simple: leave no man or woman behind; no exceptions. This obligation is something we owe to all who have served, are serving, and will serve. Some might suggest that we should not have risked lives or time to find and retrieve Bergdahl because of the potential circumstances surrounding his capture. But this commitment to our captured soldiers is unequivocal and must take place regardless of the circumstances of their capture. The Chief of Staff of the Army General Raymond Odierno has promised a thorough and transparent investigation into the circumstances surrounding Bergdahl's capture, and the Chairman of the Joint Chiefs of Staff General Martin Dempsey has been clear that that leadership "will not look away from misconduct if it occurred." But the obligation to retrieve SGT Bergdahl and the circumstances of his capture should not be conflated. Indeed, if Bergdahl did act improperly, then it is even more important that he be held accountable in the military system for his actions.

To leave any soldier behind is not only unconscionable but would damage a sacred trust with our military personnel, lead some to question our nation's commitment to our troops, and could result in a tremendous propaganda victory for our enemies. Additionally, given the ongoing transition in Afghanistan it was better to do this deal now while we have military leverage. Indeed, there was also a tremendous risk of having a captured U.S. soldier being executed on video as happened with American businessman Nick Berg Iraq in 2004 and journalist Daniel Pearl in Pakistan in 2002 – acts which not only demonstrated the brutality of our enemy but could be used to foster the recruitment of extremists and spread extremism.

Some argue that the release of 5 detainees from Guantanamo is itself a propaganda victory. In the big picture, the effects of a Taliban propaganda campaign will be short-lived and pale in comparison to recent strategic changes in Afghanistan to include a transition to Afghan security's "self reliance" and two successful rounds of elections, each of which saw around 7 million Afghans vote – 40% of them women - in open defiance of the Taliban.

While there will always be some risk posed by the release of detainees from Guantanamo Bay, these risks also held true during the Bush Administration when 532 detainees were released from Guantanamo Bay between 2002-2009, some of whom have returned to the fight. Despite the potential risks of releasing detainees from Guantanamo, there are several reasons why we should temper our concerns:

First, these detainees will be held by Qatar for the next year and will be subject to specific security measures to limit their activities and potential to become threats. As Secretary of Defense Hagel testified to the House Armed Services Committee on June 11th of this year, the Qatari government recently signed a Memoranda of Understanding with the United States that included "specific risk mitigation measures and commitments from the Government of Qatar [including] travel restrictions, monitoring, information sharing and limitations on activities, as well as other significant measures." that the Department detailed in a closed portion of the Armed Services Committee hearing.[1] As the Secretary noted, President Obama also received a personal commitment from the Emir of Qatar to uphold and enforce the security agreements outlined in this agreement.

[1] Testimony of Secretary of Defense Chuck Hagel before the House Armed Services Committee, Wednesday June 11, 2014. Available at: http://www.defense.gov/Speeches/Speech.aspx?SpeechID=1860

Second, there is not a consensus that these five individuals will inevitably return to the battlefield. A quick review of publically available materials demonstrates that recidivism is not a certainty by any means, with a rate hovering at around 10%. Statistics provided in the September 2013 unclassified summary of the "Reengagement of Detainees Formerly Held at Guantanamo Bay, Cuba" report provided by the Director of National Intelligence to Congress note that the number of detainees confirmed in re-engaging on the battlefield had been about 16.6%. A closer look reveals that of the 532 detainees released before January 22, 2009, the "confirmed" recidivism rate was around 18% but of the 71 individuals released since 2009, only 4.2% were confirmed as having returned to the battlefield.[2] A similar drop in rates has been seen with those who are suspected, but not confirmed, to have re-engaged on the battlefield. According to the DNI figures, the United States has proven more successful in the past six years than during the time between 2002-2009 in reducing recidivism rates from about 30% to about 10%. Reporting by terrorism expert Peter Bergen at the New America Foundation reinforces the notion that recidivism rates are probably even lower at around 8.7%.[3]

Third, even in the event that they do return to the battlefield, the Afghanistan of 2015 – even 2014 – is not the Afghanistan from which they were captured. Average life expectancy in Afghanistan is now 60 years vs. 42 years in 2001. At the time of the fall of the Taliban, just under a million children went to school, nearly all male. Now over 9 million children are in Afghan schools, nearly 40% of them girls. Most importantly, there is new hope – especially amongst the youth – that they can live in an Afghanistan that is at peace. Taliban insurgent networks are shattered in many places, the Afghan National Security Forces are much more capable fighters, and as already noted, the political situation in Afghanistan demonstrates that for all the Taliban's efforts, they cannot stop a peaceful transition of civilian power. The strength of the Taliban will not return because of the presence of these five individuals who have been off the battlefield for over a decade, and I am not entirely certain that they will be welcomed with open arms by their former colleagues who may not trust the fact that these individuals have been with the Americans for so long.

Furthermore, it is worth considering the potential opportunities that have been created by the completion of this exchange. Qatar has already proven an acceptable "neutral" location for the Taliban to send their representatives in search of an eventual peace within Afghanistan. We should continue to work with the Afghan government to leverage Qatari

---

[2]Unclassified Summary of DNI report to Congress IAW Sec. 307 of the Intelligence Authorization Act of FY 2012. Available at:
http://www.dni.gov/files/documents/September_2013_GTMO_Reengagement_UNCLASS_Release_FI NAL.pdf

[3] See Peter Bergen and Bailey Cahall, "How Big a Terror Risk Are Former Guantanamo Prisoners," June 8, 2014, at: www.cnn.com/2014/06/05/opinion/bergen-guantanamo-risk-of-recidivist-terrorists/index.html and Peter Bergen et al, "How Many Gitmo Alumni Take Up Arms," January 11, 2011, available at
http://newamerica.net/publications/articles/2011/how_many_gitmo_alumni_take_up_arms_42737

credibility to help move talks towards an eventual peace agreement. Indeed, retired Marine Corps General James Mattis has even suggested a military advantage to the exchange, noting that Bergdahl's release has created a "military vulnerability" for the Taliban and the Haqqani network. In short, there is now freedom for the U.S. to operate against them now that they no longer hold a U.S. prisoner.[4]

All of us would like to see an end to the conflict in Afghanistan but this will bring with it questions about the final disposition of detainees still held at Guantanamo Bay. Part of this will have to do with how lawyers define the end of "hostilities" in Afghanistan. While I cannot speak to it as a legal issue, from a political perspective it is hard to envision any comprehensive peace agreement between the Government of the Islamic Republic of Afghanistan and the Taliban that does not involve the return of the remaining Afghans at Guantanamo to Afghan government control. Therefore, it would be wise for us to generate as much political value out of the Afghan detainees while we have them. Arguably this is what was done with the five recently released. As Secretary Hagel noted in his HASC testimony, none of those detainees had been "implicated in any attacks against the United States, and we had no basis to prosecute them in a federal court or military commission."[5] The alternative is to keep them in confinement forever without any charges.

Additionally, as history has shown, an exchange of prisoners does not have to wait until after a war ends but can happen as wars draw to a close, as part of potential or actual negotiations and before the final armistice or peace-treaties are completed. For example, while the Korean War armistice was not signed until the end of July 1953, both sides had already conducted Operation "Little Switch," (April 20 - May 3, 1953) where 684 U.N. sick and wounded troops (including 149 Americans) were exchanged for 1,030 Chinese and 5,194 Korean troops. Indeed, major fighting continued after this exchange of prisoners including the Battle of Pork Chop Hill, engagements in the Kumsong River Salient, as well as some of the largest U.S. Navy and Marine Corps air operations of the war. Even during the Second World War, there is a record of at least one exchange prior to the conclusion of hostilities, in this case, in November 1944, when A. Gerow Hodges, an International Red Cross worker detailed to the U.S. 94th Division, was able to convince German military authorities to swap 149 American POWs for a like number of German prisoners.[6]

---

[4] General James Mattis on CNN's "State of the Union," June 8 2014. Available at: http://transcripts.cnn.com/TRANSCRIPTS/1406/08/sotu.01.html

[5] Hagel testimony, http://www.defense.gov/Speeches/Speech.aspx?SpeechID=1860

[6] Then Senator Hillary Clinton made mention of this prisoner exchange during remarks on the Senate floor on Wednesday, November 7, 2007. See Congressional Record, Volume 153, Number 172, Wednesday, November 7, 2007 [Senate], Pages S14057-14058. http://www.gpo.gov/fdsys/pkg/CREC-2007-11-07/html/CREC-2007-11-07-pt1-PgS14057-3.htm For a more detailed news account of this event see Don Moore, "Jewish POWs Swapped By Germans in World War II," blog posting available at http://donmooreswartales.com/2010/05/12/harry-glixon/

Some question whether the recent prisoner exchange created a precedent that will engager the lives of U.S. personnel and has broken from past practice of not negotiating with terrorists. I think this assessment is too simple and in some cases disregards historical precedent. First, the threat of kidnapping to U.S. members of the armed forces, diplomats, and citizens has long been the case in Afghanistan, and our forces have been prepared for that throughout over a dozen years of conflict in Afghanistan. Indeed, I felt this was my own greatest threat during my military and civilian service in Afghanistan. There is no reason to think that this calculus will be altered by the recent exchange. In short, terrorists and insurgents with whom we are at war have wanted to kidnap Americans before and will most certainly keep trying to in the future.

The deal to retrieve SGT Bergdahl was a prisoner exchange, not a negotiation with terrorists. But that said it is important to note that the popular view that the United States does not negotiate with insurgents, terrorists, or even state sponsors of terrorism is not historically accurate. In terms of the Taliban alone, the United States has been talking and negotiating with the Taliban for some time in recognition that the war in Afghanistan cannot end without a political settlement.[7] A quick review of history illustrates that at particular times, the United States has found it necessary to negotiate with terrorists and state-sponsors of terrorism. In 1968, United States negotiated the North Korean government in 1968 to obtain the release of 83 American personnel on the *USS Pueblo* that had been boarded and captured by the North Koreans.[8] As former State Department official Mitchell Reiss has noted in his book *Negotiating with Evil*, President Nixon pressured allies, including Israel, to release prisoners as part of negotiations with the Popular Front for the Liberation of Palestine in order to resolve the hijacking of two hijacked airliners; the Iran hostage crisis of 1979-1981 was resolved in part by the agreement to unfreeze $8 billion in frozen Iranian assets; and of course, there was the "arms for hostages" deal negotiated by the Reagan Administration as part of what eventually become the Iran-Contra affair.[9] Likewise, while the negotiations were rather one-sided, Ambassador Robert Oakley did meet with the late Somali Warlord, Mohammad Farah Aideed to secure the release of Chief Warrant Officer Michael Durant who was held in captivity after the Battle of Mogadishu in October 1993.[10]

---

[7] See Ambassador Marc Grossman, "Talking to the Taliban 2010-2011 – A Reflection," PRISM, Volume 4, Number 4, Center for Complex Operations, National Defense University, Washington DC. Available at: http://cco.dodlive.mil/files/2014/04/Talking_To_the_Taliban.pdf

[8] For a short review of the experiences of the crew of the *USS Pueblo* in captivity see. CAPT Raymond C. Spaulding, "Some Experiences Reported by the Crew of the USS *Pueblo* and American Prisoners of War from Vietnam," January 1975. Available at http://www.history.navy.mil/library/special/pueblo.htm

[9] See Alan Gomez, "Is it Ever Right to Negotiate With Terrorists," USA Today, June 2nd 2014. Available at: http://www.usatoday.com/story/news/world/2014/06/01/bergdahl-release-taliban-prisoner-trade/9835759/

[10] See Dan Lamothe, "Why Black Hawk Down Prisoner Release is Different Than Bowe Bergdahl's," *Washington Post*, June 11, 2014.

Other nations have done this as well – Margaret Thatcher negotiated secretly with the Irish Republican Army and while Israel has at times famously said it will not negotiate with terrorists, we know that successive Israeli administrations have made prisoner exchanges – at times trading a thousand prisoners for just a few Israeli soldiers. But in all these cases it is important to distinguish between those situations more akin to what is expected in war – e.g. a prisoner exchange, part of a complex series of counterinsurgency initiatives, . In other words, negotiating with a terrorist group or a state-sponsor of terrorism does not necessarily equate to paying ransom for hostages.

I understand the disappointment we feel in the stories coming out about Sergeant Bowe Bergdahl, and I understand the anger felt by some of his comrades who feel that he deliberately left his post. If I were them, I might feel the same way. But the truth is that we do not know the truth. Unfortunately, the process to determine it is impacted by all the speculation in a public setting. In our nation of laws the presumption of innocence is sacrosanct, an age old principal that demands, even if we believe with all our being otherwise, that people are innocent until proven guilty. Now that the Department of Defense has announced its intent to have Maj. General Dahl lead an investigation of the facts and circumstances surrounding Sergeant Berghdal's disappearance and capture, it is imperative to preserve the integrity of that investigation – it must be thorough and allowed to take place without politics or partisanship.[11] Without it we are unlikely to ever have accountability.

We may not like it, but in the end, foreign affairs and national security policy are often about juggling bad options and finding the least worst of these options; there are rarely simple solutions. The decision to exchange Sergeant Bergdahl may be imperfect, but it my mind, it represented the right approach to balancing national security security needs and does not in any way prevent the United States from continuing to prosecute a war with our Afghan partners against the Taliban nor does it appreciably increase the risk of new threats. We have been negotiating with the Taliban to find a solution in Afghanistan and we have precedents for negotiating with groups such as the Taliban for prisoner exchanges. The potential threat posed by these detainees must be looked at within the context of the Afghanistan to which they will return. Regardless, we never leave our soldiers behind.

Thank you again Mr. Chairman and Madam Chairwoman for inviting me to testify today and I am pleased to answer any questions you may have.

---

http://www.washingtonpost.com/news/checkpoint/wp/2014/06/11/why-the-black-hawk-down-prisoner-release-is-different-than-bowe-bergdahls/

[11] Department of Defense Press Release, June 16, 2014.
http://www.defense.gov/Releases/Release.aspx?ReleaseID=16776

Mr. POE. Thank all of you all for your testimony. We'll now go to questions by the individual members. I recognize myself for 5 minutes.

There are several issues that have come to light during this hearing, the first one is Sergeant Bergdahl, why did he leave his post, and what's going to happen to him in the future? The second would be those that looked for him, what happened to some of them, and what did the government, the U.S. Army tell those who lost sons looking for him?

There is the issue of do we negotiate with terrorists or do we not negotiate with terrorists? What is the foreign policy of the United States? Maybe one of you could come up with the answer to that question.

And then there's the Taliban Five, or as Mr. Waltz has called them, the Taliban war cabinet, I believe is what the term was. Who are the folks, and why were they in GITMO in the first place, and what are they going to do in the future? So, those are the four issues that I want to address.

Let's start with you, Mr. Andrews. What did the Army tell you about the way your son was killed?

Mr. ANDREWS. They said that they were searching for a high-ranking Taliban, and had gone to this bazaar to search for him. And because of—this was actually in the Silver Star commendation, but because they had so many problems with IEDs on the road, that instead of coming in from the south, they sent them around to come in from the north.

Mr. POE. Excuse me for interrupting, but they told you they were—your son was looking for a Taliban commander of some type?

Mr. ANDREWS. Bergdahl was never mentioned.

Mr. POE. All right. When did you learn that that was not true?

Mr. ANDREWS. Last Saturday.

Mr. POE. Were you ever instructed, or asked, or told by the U.S. Army to sign a confidentiality agreement not to tell anybody about what you were told by the Army?

Mr. ANDREWS. I was not, but the soldiers who contacted my wife were asked to sign a non-disclosure agreement, they said.

Mr. POE. All right. Sergeant Full, you obviously are very passionate about your testimony. Were members of the United States military killed looking for Bergdahl?

Mr. FULL. I don't know. What I do know is we were told that we wouldn't be in certain areas before he went and deserted us. So, if he wouldn't have deserted us we, probably—those people wouldn't have been in those places where they were killed on that day. They would have been somewhere else, they would have been in a different section of Afghanistan.

Mr. POE. Mr. Waltz, do you want to weigh in on that specific question?

Mr. WALTZ. Mr. Chairman, I can't draw, and I don't know of anyone that can draw a direct line, but I can tell you to the best of my knowledge every unit, particularly in Paktika Province where Specialist Full was located, but also mine, and Khost, and the Zorani Provinces in Ghazni were dedicated to that search. If someone was killed during that specific amount of time, unless they tripped and hit their head on the way to the mess hall, they were out looking for Sergeant Bergdahl.

Mr. POE. The Taliban war cabinet, Mr. Waltz, you indicated a lot of concern about who these guys are. One of them, even the United Nations has indicted one of them for war crimes. Who are these people? Americans are really not sure, they don't know who these type folks are.

Mr. WALTZ. Well, Mr. Chairman, we have—we've released now the Taliban's Deputy Minister of Defense, a senior operative in their intelligence service that was responsible for migrating al-Qaeda intelligence tactics over the Taliban. We have released the former Taliban governor of Herat, which is the westernmost province on the border with Iran and was responsible for liaising with the Iranian Government on behalf of the Taliban. And we released gentlemen that were wanted for war crimes for literally massacring thousands of the ethnic minority that are Shia. We look at the sectarian violence going on across the Middle East, I wouldn't call that necessarily a wise move.

These gentlemen—the question I can't get anyone to ask that was involved with this, and I've talked to a number, is why did the Taliban pick those five? Out of all of the spectrum of folks they could have chosen out of Guantanamo, why did we give them essentially their top five draft picks?

Mr. POE. And one follow-up question on that. Understanding the agreement, Qatar is supposed to supervise them, but the supervision or house arrest, if you will, is for just 1 year. Is that your understanding of the deal that was made?

Mr. WALTZ. That's my understanding, Mr. Chairman. And, frankly, I think some of the details of what they can or can't do in the next year are almost moot. The fact is it's only for a year.

Mr. POE. Last question. Dr. Jacobson, we've heard this through the media. The Lovelady family in Texas was told that the United States doesn't negotiate with terrorists. Their son was later killed in the Algerian attack. Does the United States have a policy that we don't negotiate with terrorists, or we don't have a policy?

Mr. JACOBSON. What I can tell you is that I don't believe that the Bergdahl exchange is an example of negotiating with terrorists. I believe it is an exchange of prisoners, something that we've seen historically toward the end of war.

Mr. POE. Thank you very much. The Chair will now recognize the ranking member, the gentleman from California, Mr. Sherman, for 5 minutes.

Mr. SHERMAN. Let me first put to rest this absurd argument that these five Taliban prisoners would have to have been released under the laws of war when we concluded combat operations in 2014, or when we were down to a couple of hundred trainers in 2016. I'm pleased to note for our record that just last week the General Counsel of the Department of Defense, Steve Preston, testified there that we would continue to have a legal right to hold Taliban prisoners, not just with the conclusion of war in Afghanistan, but until the broader battle defined under the AUMF was concluded.

We're going to continue to have American trainers in Afghanistan for many, many years. The Taliban soldiers will try to kill

48

those trainers. The laws of war do not require us to augment the forces trying to wage war against our trainers or against the Afghan Government. We are at war with the Taliban for as long as they are allied with terrorist organizations waging war against the United States, or as long as the Taliban is waging war against the government in Afghanistan.

Mr. Jacobson, I've got a number of questions. I'm hoping you'll be able to answer them very succinctly in some cases with a yes or no. We're told that some of these five released are "wanted by the U.N. for war crimes." Does the U.N. have a process by which anyone can be wanted by the U.N. for war crimes? Have they ever indicted anybody? Do they have a process to indict anybody?

Mr. JACOBSON. I'm unaware of that, and I understand that there is some debate over how that came in some of the DoD documents, and where that came from.

Mr. SHERMAN. There are many urban legends in foreign policy. Are any of these five under indictment from the International Criminal Court or any other recognized body that focuses on war crimes?

Mr. JACOBSON. You would have to ask the Department of State, or you'd have to ask the International——

Mr. SHERMAN. Are you aware——

Mr. JACOBSON. I'm not aware, no.

Mr. SHERMAN. And I did ask you to research this, didn't I?

Mr. JACOBSON. What I think is important, Congressman, is understanding, again, this context. These individuals are dangerous but they are simply not going back to that same battlefield from which they were captured.

Mr. SHERMAN. I've got very limited time. I want to go on to something else. The question arises whether continued patrols should have been made to try to retrieve Sergeant Bergdahl. I should note for the record here that Senators Toomey, Burr, and Senate Republican Leader Mitch McConnell, along with eight Republican members of the House, at a time when we already knew the mysterious circumstances of Bergdahl's departure, and that this was widely published put forward a resolution stating that "abandoning the search efforts for members of the armed forces who are missing or captured is unacceptable." At the time, there was only one member of our armed services missing or captured, and these fine Members of Congress, House, and Senate knew full well that those additional patrols that they were demanding would be dangerous for our armed forces.

I should also point out that as to whether this deal was a good deal, it was Senator McCain who knew exactly the parameters of this deal, except for the details, that it was these five for one named Bergdahl because the possible outlines of this deal were published on the front page of the Washington Post on February 17th, and in that context on February 18th Senator McCain said he was for the deal if the details were correct. Now, maybe the details don't meet his specifications, but it is, indeed, a close call whether this five for one deal was or was not in the national security interest of the United States.

We are told that it is somehow news that we've revealed to the Taliban that we care about our prisoners. The only other democracy to have soldiers captured in the Middle East to my knowledge is Israel. Dr. Jacobson, what were the Israelis willing to do to get back Sergeant Major Gilad Shalit?

Mr. JACOBSON. I don't want to mistake the details of that particular case, but what I am aware of is at times the Israelis have exchanged over 1,000 prisoners for one individual, and also they've exchanged prisoners for the remains of their fallen.

Mr. SHERMAN. So, anyone observing the practices of democracies doing battle in the Middle East would reach the conclusion that if you could capture somebody, democracies have a particular need to try to get that person back and are willing to make extraordinary concessions, as you pointed out, sometimes 1,000 to 1.

Mr. JACOBSON. I don't think anyone would disagree with the point that our democracy has shown that it cares a great deal about our men and women who have been left behind and captured.

Mr. SHERMAN. And, finally, as to these five released Taliban, their battlefield experience is from 2001. Were the tactics that they're familiar with near as good as the tactics used by the Taliban today?

Mr. JACOBSON. Unfortunately, in my opinion the insurgents in Afghanistan have evolved tremendously since that period in 2001 in terms of their tactics.

Mr. POE. Mr. Sherman's time has expired. The Chair recognizes the gentleman from Illinois, Mr. Kinzinger, for 5 minutes.

Mr. KINZINGER. Thank you, Mr. Chairman. And, again, thank you all for being here. I just, you know, again we're going to the idea of let's point out everybody that ever said anything about releasing this one person and, therefore, the administration made the right decision because others said it.

I'd be remiss if I didn't make a bigger point here on the Afghanistan issue, which is the President has announced that in January 2017, all American troops will be out of Afghanistan. And, you know, that's fine for him to make that decision, but I would just point people to what's happening in Iraq today as a precursor of what's going to happen in Afghanistan if that occurs. But, again, we're here for the specific issues. And, again, I want to thank all of you for being here.

Let me ask a question to the Specialist. What do you think— when you were in training and you heard this idea of your country will never leave you behind, and it's something that as members of the armed forces we take very seriously, and something that we take a great deal of comfort in. When you heard that, what is your understanding of your country will never leave you behind mean? What does that guarantee in your mind, and is that an idea that they will release five or 1,000 terrorists to get you back? What is it that that meant to you, Specialist?

Mr.FULL. Well, what it means to me is, you know, I put my nation first when I volunteered to serve the United States Army in the time of war. So, by putting them first, they would put me first to a certain extent. But I keep hearing, you know, we shall leave no man behind because we can trade with another nation, and it's done in all these previous wars, but Taliban is not a nation. They're a terrorist organization, so is the Haqqani Network who helped Bowe Bergdahl. From what I gathered from it, it was always leave no honorable man behind, not leave no man behind.

Mr. KINZINGER. And do you believe—so, you may be in touch with folks that are still in Afghanistan or, obviously, people you served with. And I'll ask the four of you, and you can expand on this, Specialist, because we want—the other three I'll ask to keep fairly short.

Do you believe that the release of Bergdahl from the Taliban and the subsequent video they put out, obviously, has to have some meaning showing, i.e., the American helicopter leaving and, in essence, withdrawing from the area. Do you believe that was a propaganda victory or a propaganda defeat for the Taliban, this exchange? And what do you think that does to the heart of the soldier that saw this happen, Specialist?

Mr. FULL. I think it's a propaganda victory for the Taliban on account of now we're kind of a direct—only traded one for five. It's simple math.

Mr. KINZINGER. And do you sense that this will help or hurt the Taliban's recruiting effort to recruit people to kill Americans, and to kill Afghans who have put their lives on the line to build a strong and stable country?

Mr. FULL. I would assume it would help them, and not hurt them.

Mr. KINZINGER. Mr. Andrews, what's your thought on that question?

Mr. ANDREWS. From what I can see, it is a victory propaganda-wise for the Taliban. They won, you know, it is the way it looks like when you see the footage, so I think it benefitted the Taliban greatly. I think it also put soldiers more in danger of being captured because the rewards are more for getting one and trading them rather than——

Mr. KINZINGER. Thank you. Mr. Waltz, and Mr. Jacobson, please, very quickly if you guys could just respond either yes or no, basically.

Mr. WALTZ. Just very quickly, Mullah Omar, the leader of the Taliban, considered it a victory and stated so as soon as he received his five top commanders back.

Mr. JACOBSON. I don't trust Mullah Omar, so I would say it pales by comparison to the video that could have taken place with one of our soldiers being beheaded like we saw with Nick Berg or with Daniel Pearl.

Mr. KINZINGER. Well, that's an interesting twist. So, your twist is you don't trust this guy; therefore, him saying that it was a victory for his organization is probably a lie. And, I mean, that's kind of surprising to me, because I think if it was not a victory for them, they probably wouldn't have said anything. They released a video and they probably would have sat back and been very quiet about it, so that's an interesting spin. You have a right to your opinion, but I think that was an interesting take that the other three do not share.

And do you believe, Specialist, do you believe he intentionally left his post? And do you have a sense as to why he might have intentionally left?

Mr. FULL. Yes, I do believe he left without a doubt. We knew within 1 hour, 2 hours that he had deserted. I don't know why he did it. He, obviously, had a plan. It was premeditated. Why would you ship all your items home in the middle of a deployment? So, with the emails and other questions he asked us, connecting the dots later, yes, he deserted without a doubt.

Mr. KINZINGER. So, I get—and thank you. And while I get, you know, some folks saying well, we need to wait to have this adjudicated in courts, and I understand the idea of that. The reality is, we know that Sergeant Bergdahl left his post. We know it.

Now, was he in full mental state? I guess that can be determined, but there are a lot of people that have had mental challenges with dealing with what happened in Afghanistan and Iraq that still do not leave their brothers and sisters behind in combat. So, with that, Mr. Chairman, I thank the witnesses, and I yield back.

Mr. POE. The gentleman yields back. The Chair recognizes the gentleman from Florida, Mr. Deutch, for 5 minutes.

Mr. DEUTCH. Thank you, Mr. Chairman.

Mr. Waltz, Sergeant Bergdahl was designated missing and captured, right, at the time?

Mr. WALTZ. My understanding, sir, is he was designated missing and a prisoner of war, and that's why he was since promoted in absentia. That confers a number of benefits.

Mr. DEUTCH. And, Dr. Jacobson, how is that determination made?

Mr. JACOBSON. Well, that determination was made by the Department of Defense. I don't know the specific details, what they would have to go through, but I would agree with—my understanding is the same as Mike's.

Mr. DEUTCH. For both of you, what process—I understand, as I said in my opening comments, and now it has been confirmed by some of the comments by my colleagues, some of them know what happened. They have reached a conclusion. It was obvious, we're told. But what does the military actually do to reach the same conclusion? What steps does the military take in determining whether someone who is determined to be missing is actually—has actually deserted? Mr. Waltz?

Mr. WALTZ. Congressman, if I—I think the key point here is that what the military has done to date has been initial and, therefore, incomplete. They have not done a full investigation and, therefore, I'm not sure how one would draw a full conclusion as to what they think—what we think happened.

Mr. DEUTCH. But how do they—do you have any further insight? It seems very easy from what a lot of elected officials said, it's not that hard to figure out. He's a deserter and, apparently, we shouldn't have made this deal. Well, what's the military done to reach that same conclusion?

Mr. WALTZ. Sir, my understanding of the deal at the time was that a 15–6 or some type of investigation under UCMJ was conducted. A number of the folks that were on site were interviewed, and the reason that investigation was not closed was they needed to interview the subject at hand, who was obviously missing.

Mr. DEUTCH. And if that investigation continues, what might they learn, Dr. Jacobson? What could they learn during that investigation?

Mr. JACOBSON. From what I have seen in the press so far, a great deal has come out. For example, we have seen information come out that perhaps Sergeant Bergdahl tried to escape several times, which forced his captors to put him into isolation. We've now seen reports about Sergeant Bergdahl's prior enlistment in the Coast Guard.

I walk away with more questions from what I've seen come out so far. We've even seen today in testimony, what type of person, was Sergeant Bergdahl? So, again, more questions, which is exactly why there needs to be a full investigation of the circumstances surrounding his capture.

Mr. DEUTCH. Dr. Jacobson, Mr. Waltz, what happens if my colleagues are wrong? What happens if the military completes its investigation and determines any one of a thousand different things happened, and that Sergeant Bergdahl was, in fact, missing and a prisoner of war, not a deserter? Can you speak to that?

Mr. JACOBSON. Let me speak to it. Mike might have some other comments, but my concern is if we look back at what happened to many of our prisoners of war during the Korean War and during the Vietnam War, many were accused of collaboration, not acting properly. In fact, Senator McCain was at the forefront of insuring that many of those records were sealed until proper investigations could be done, because our enemies want us to think that certain things happened. And I'm not suggesting one way or another that this happened during the Bergdahl case, but that's why we have to be careful so we don't impugn those who didn't do wrong.

Mr. DEUTCH. I have a minute left, let me just cut to the chase. If the military conducts its full investigation and determines that Sergeant Bergdahl is a deserter, what's the penalty for that?

Mr. WALTZ. Sir, in wartime, and there's some debate whether this has been officially declared as a war. In wartime, that could be punishable up to death. There are various forms of UCMJ punishment obviously less than that. But to your point, sir, there's been a lot of discussion of rush to judgment, and I would postulate at least I would have reacted very differently. I know Specialist Full would have reacted very differently if this had been handled appropriately in the first few days after his release with the accusations of hero and served with distinction and what have you.

Mr. DEUTCH. Mr. Waltz, I'm grateful for the distinction in your approach. In all sincerity, I'm glad you made that comment. I would just finish with this last question. As you pointed out, there are a whole range of punishments from—under the Uniform Code of Military Justice. Is one of those punishments subcontracted out to the Taliban to decide how to punish someone? I yield back, Mr. Chairman.

Mr. POE. You may answer the question yes or no, if you can.

Mr. WALTZ. Mr. Chairman, I'm not sure I understand the question.

Mr. POE. Okay. The gentleman does yield back his time. The Chair will recognize the gentleman from Arkansas, Mr. Cotton, for 5 minutes.

53

Mr. COTTON. Mr. and Mrs. Andrews, I am deeply sorry for your loss. Nothing will bring back your son, Darryn, but hopefully the truth, which I'd like to get at in the next 5 minutes, will help salve the wounds that no doubt are still with you.

For the record, I'd like to corroborate what Specialist Full and Mr. Waltz have said that impact our missions across Afghanistan. I was in Laughman Province which is part of a thing called N2KL, Nuristan and Kunar, through Laughman Province. We saw the diversion of air assets to search for Private Bergdahl.

Second, I'd also like to stipulate for the record that if there were no doubt that Private Bergdahl had been captured heroically on the field of battle trying to save his fellow Americans, I would still think trading five senior Taliban commanders was a bad idea.

Likewise, even though all evidence points toward his desertion, it would still be the right thing to do to try to rescue him as Specialist Full and Lieutenant Andrews did. And, of course, he deserves his day in court according to this chain of command, or now unlawful command influence of this President, or any civilian leaders or general officers in the Pentagon.

Now, Mr. Jacobson, would you trade Khalid Sheik Mohammed for Private Bergdahl?

Mr. JACOBSON. Congressman, I mean, that was——

Mr. COTTON. Reclaiming my time, it's a simple yes or no question.

Mr. JACOBSON. I don't think that there are simple yes or no questions like that in war.

Mr. COTTON. Reclaiming my time, I gather by your unwillingness to answer the question you realize that you cannot answer it. Tony Blinken, the present Senior Deputy Security Advisor said that he would not. So, I guess that means under those circumstances the President would have been leaving Private Bergdahl behind.

Now, moving to Specialist Full, you say in your statement that you are part of Alpha Team. Were you on the same team as Private Bergdahl?

Mr. FULL. Same platoon, same squad, same team.

Mr. COTTON. Okay. So, down to the lowest level, those of you don't know, that's a four-man fire team.

Mr. FULL. We were one man short, so it was just——

Mr. COTTON. Were you his team leader at the time?

Mr. FULL. No, I was not.

Mr. COTTON. Okay. So, you are among the one or two people on the team who had been working most closely with him and seen him in action day, after day, after day.

Mr. FULL. Yes.

Mr. COTTON. Okay. I've heard numerous reports that Private Bergdahl sought out and had civilian Afghanistan friends, something I saw commonly in Afghanistan and Iraq, soldiers engaging in conversation, oftentimes innocent with children, maybe dining on base with Afghan security officers. Is that an accurate report, that he had these civilian friends in and around OP MEST?

Mr. FULL. Yes.

Mr. COTTON. Okay. You testified, or you stated in your testimony a cleric and teacher saw him looking, roaming as to the children, and you heard over the radio the interpreter that an American was looking for someone in the village who spoke English, and wanted to talk to the Taliban. If he had numerous civilian Afghan friends, is it curious to you that he would ask them where the Taliban is rather than simply hide out with him?

Mr. FULL. I'm not sure I understand the question.

Mr. COTTON. So, if Private Bergdahl left his post and attempted, as you say, to wander across the mountains perhaps to India, do you think it's curious that he wouldn't be asking his friends in Afghanistan where the Taliban is rather than just hanging out in a hideout with his friends?

Mr. FULL. Yes.

Mr. COTTON. Tactics, techniques and procedures, TTPs, that describes how we conduct operations, what is the established order for conducting any particular task or operation in the Army. Is that correct?

Mr. FULL. Yes.

Mr. COTTON. In the missions after Private Bergdahl's disappearance did it appear that the Afghan enemy had greater knowledge of your unit's TTPs, such as where you park after an IED, or how you react in ambush?

Mr. FULL. I don't know if they had greater knowledge after he did disappear. I don't know if another player moved into the area or whatnot, but after he did disappear, yes, the ambushes picked up, cover and concealment was used. They hit us hard after he left. IEDs were moved in different directions, and they were, instead of taking a tire or a front end off a vehicle, they were hitting direct hits on the vehicles.

Mr. COTTON. And that would be consistent with Private Bergdahl being held in captivity by the Taliban, Haqqani Network and breaking under interrogation and sharing those TTPs. Correct?

Mr. FULL. I don't know. I wasn't there while he was held under captivity. I don't know what he told them. I wasn't there.

Mr. COTTON. It could also be consistent with the fact that he willingly shared those TTPs with the Taliban and Haqqani Network. Correct?

Mr. FULL. Like I said, I don't know what he told them, what he didn't tell them. I wasn't there.

Mr. COTTON. When you were conducting missions in the days and weeks after his disappearance did any of your NCOs or your team leader or company commander raise the possibility that Private Bergdahl might be a security risk himself if you were to find him on the battlefield?

Mr. FULL. Our main focus at that point was just trying to find him and get him back. It didn't matter how, who, or when, but that was our main focus from the time he left until about 2½ months later, every day trying to find this guy.

Mr. COTTON. Were you asked to sign a non-disclosure agreement as part of your Article 15–6 investigation?

Mr. FULL. I was asked to sign a media gag order. There was other people in my platoon that were asked to sign an official NDA with, you know, a field grade officer present to witness them signing.

Mr. COTTON. Mr. Waltz——

Mr. POE. The gentleman's time has expired. The Chair will recognize the gentleman from Rhode Island, Mr. Cicilline, for 5 minutes.

Mr. CICILLINE. Thank you, Mr. Chairman.

Mr. Jacobson, obviously we've heard testimony today and there have been some reports of some unusual behavior attributed to Sergeant Bergdahl. And, obviously, our great American soldiers overwhelmingly are able to sustain the stresses and difficulties of combat without exhibiting unusual behavior that had been described both during this hearing and in the media. And is there a system or process in place to evaluate the behavior of a soldier to make a determination as to whether or not it's related to the combat operations, or related to his or her service?

Mr. JACOBSON. Congressman, speaking from my own experience there were—the first line of defense when you have a soldier who's a problem or not doing things right is his chain of command. That would include their NCOs and the officers above them. There are also—during my time in Afghanistan there were a great—there was a great deal of effort expended to make sure that there were preventive mental health clinics and places where soldiers could go. I cannot speak to the specifics of any of this with regards to Bergdahl, though.

Mr. CICILLINE. But there's a system in place to monitor members of the armed forces to insure that we're understanding the impact of being in combat and the stresses of their service.

Mr. JACOBSON. That's my understanding, especially over the last decade.

Mr. CICILLINE. And in addition to that, one of the reasons we—there's a process to conduct a hearing and an investigation, and a review of those facts to make a determination as to whether or not someone has deserted, or something else is going on. Is that right?

Mr. JACOBSON. Absolutely.

Mr. CICILLINE. And there is a process that will happen, in fact, in this case as it relates to this individual?

Mr. JACOBSON. In fact, the Department of Defense earlier this week announced that it will be a Two Star General who will be leading the overall investigation. We've heard Army Chief of Staff Odierno say that there will a full investigation, and that was echoed by the Chairman of the Joints Chief of Staff, General Martin Dempsey.

Mr. CICILLINE. So, in addition to that we have this other principle about insuring that we leave no soldier behind as part of kind of the warrior ethos, as part of the soldier's creed. It's a deeply held American belief and practice that we leave no soldier behind, and we do everything we can to secure the release of any American who's caught in time of war. Correct?

Mr. JACOBSON. That is something that I believe in. That is something that I think that even if you don't like the circumstances of someone being captured you believe it's necessary to go and get them, leave no one behind.

Mr. CICILLINE. So, why wouldn't we do this hearing, investigation, and all the kinds of things that are going to happen now before we secure the release of an American? Isn't that what—couldn't we do it that way?

Mr. JACOBSON. I'm not sure I understand your question.

Mr. CICILLINE. My point is, we can't conduct an investigation, the kind of investigation that is required and that is underway prior to securing the release of the prisoner of war in most instances.

Mr. JACOBSON. I think that would be very difficult because you want to interview the individual captured. That's why, as I said before, there was an initial investigation that was by definition incomplete.

Mr. CICILLINE. So, it makes sense then that we do everything we can to secure the release of every American prisoner of war. And then if, in fact, an investigation proves that they have done something improper or engaged in some misconduct they will, of course, be required—be punished in the appropriate way. And in this case if, in fact, this individual turns out to be having deserted under the Military Code of Justice he could up to, you said, a death sentence.

Mr. JACOBSON. Yes, I think—now, I understand that death is a possible punishment, too. I would note that the last American deserter prosecuted, Charles Jenkins, he had left his post on a DMZ in Korea, the demilitarized zone in Korea in the '60s. When he came back to the United States 2006–2008 time frame he was court-martialed, sentenced to 26 days confinement, and then given a dishonorable discharge. That's a range, or that comes after the investigation and after charges are referred and there is a trial.

Mr. CICILLINE. And, Dr. Jacobson, my final question is what do you think the impact would be on our American military if our men and women did not know that this country was committed to securing their release and to undertaking every imaginable effort to bring them home?

Mr. JACOBSON. I think, first, that that would shatter the bonds of trust between the soldiers and the American people, and the chain of command. Secondly, I think that it would be an enormous propaganda coup for our enemies when they have these people in captivity that we don't care about. It would signal in many ways that we no longer are committed to our men and women in uniform.

Mr. CICILLINE. Thank you, Dr. Jacobson. I yield back, Mr. Chairman.

Mr. POE. The gentleman yields back the time. The Chair recognizes the gentleman from California, Mr. Cook, Colonel Cook, for 5 minutes.

Mr. COOK. Thank you, Mr. Chairman.

Mr. Andrews, I know it's tough to be here. As someone who's been in combat, the second hardest duty, I know probably the hardest duty is to actually go up to the parents or the spouses and then to tell them their son or daughter is no longer with them. It is very tough what you're going through. You have my heartfelt condolences.

Specialist, if you could bear with me some of the questions. I understand that his weapon was left behind?

Mr. FULL. That is correct.

Mr. COOK. All his ammunition?

Mr. FULL. Ammunition, night vision, his plate carrier.

Mr. COOK. Night vision device was left behind?

Mr. FULL. Yes, all sensitive items were left behind. A couple of days before that he had asked another platoon member what would happen if one of his sensitive items went missing, would that certain soldier be in trouble? That certain soldier responded with yes, so Bergdahl left all his sensitive items.

Mr. COOK. Did he have access to radio freqs?

Mr. FULL. He would, but he didn't have a radio with him.

Mr. COOK. No, but just the frequencies themselves, they were all pre-programmed into the radio?

Mr. FULL. Yes. Standard procedure when DUSTWAN happens you change your radio frequency.

Mr. COOK. Okay. Any maps or GPS systems at all that went with him, or was that all left behind?

Mr. FULL. I don't know if he had a map on him, but GPS would be sensitive equipment. He didn't have that.

Mr. COOK. Okay. I think there's been a lot of talk about desertion and everything else. Correct me if I'm wrong, but usually in a situation like that desertion is pretty much an admin term because one of the elements that you have to prove is permanent desertion. So, an individual that would disappear from the unit, I don't know, all the instances that I had, and I was a legal officer when I came back from—it's normally just unauthorized absence. That's one of the charges because you have to prove permanent desertion from the unit. Am I correct or incorrect on that?

Mr. FULL. That is correct. AWOL also turns into desertion after 30 days.

Mr. COOK. Administratively, normally, so that they're carried on that. But once they turn themselves in or what have you, that turns into—okay.

A couple of things in terms of just trust in the unit. I get the impression that the unit itself, and I really believe in the Code of Conduct. I believe in taking care of everybody in the unit, and to give your life for somebody like that. But I get the feeling that you lost full trust and confidence in that individual that he would be on your right flank or your left flank. In other words——

Mr. FULL. As far as the rest of the platoon?

Mr. COOK. No, you, and if you could—if you had any opinions what the feeling of the rest of the platoon is?

Mr. FULL. Well, the rest of the platoon, we're brothers. None of the rest of us walked off on our own free will.

Mr. COOK. No, but I—the attitude of this individual that was missing in action.

Mr. FULL. Well, he walked off on his own accord. If he never would have walked off, he never would have been held in captivity. The rest of us fought for the guy to our left and our right, and in front and back. And I don't know he felt about us but we all felt strongly that we would give our lives for him.

Mr. COOK. Okay. In terms of the Taliban, I'm not going to go into the surprise, you know, that you weren't notified, but just an impact on a combat unit that is fighting that organization and then suddenly for whatever reason that five of their top leaders, five of the ones that call the strategy, five of the ones that kill Americans, five of the ones that are involved in terrorism, are released. What kind of psychological impact do you think that would have for the unit aside from Bergdahl?

Mr. FULL. Well, if my high-ranking members in my organization were released back to me, I'd feel pretty good about getting my top level guys back, personally.

Mr. COOK. I understand that, but from the standpoint of the fact that the Taliban, basically the enemy that you're trying to track down, find, and everything else, that the impact that hey, they're back there calling the shots. Would that have a demoralizing impact on the unit if you were still with that unit, of course?

Mr. FULL. Oh, no. The American forces are going to do whatever they can every single day, do what they're supposed to do. I don't think they're really worried about anybody else.

Mr. COOK. Okay. Mr. Waltz, in terms of permanent impact on policy in regards, have we set a precedent by doing this in regards to all the other terrorist groups?

Mr. WALTZ. I believe we have, Congressman. I believe we've set a dangerous precedent, and I'd encourage this body to look closely at future efforts toward release and calls to close Guantanamo. We had these gentlemen detained. Men and women gave their lives to detain them. Now, unfortunately, I believe men and women will give their lives to capture or kill them once again.

Mr. COOK. Thank you. And I want to thank the panel. I yield back.

Mr. POE. The gentleman yields back his time. The Chair recognizes the gentleman from California, Mr. Vargas, for 5 minutes.

Mr. VARGAS. Mr. Chairman, thank you very much. And, again, thank you for holding this hearing. I want to add my condolences, too, to the Andrews family and, sir, to yourself and to your wife. And I hope that the chemotherapy that we've heard about just a little while ago is successful, sir. And your son, obviously, clearly was a hero, and thank God for him. And Specialist Full, too, we want to thank you. I want to thank you for your service to our nation. Mr. Waltz, you also, obviously, for the great service you've got. Mr. Jacobson, I want to ask you a little bit because earlier on everyone was thanked for their service except for you. Do you remember that? You were kind of cut off? You weren't thanked for your service. Do you remember that?

Mr. JACOBSON. I heard a lot of thanks for service.

Mr. VARGAS. Okay. What was your service, because at one point everyone was thanked except for you. I thought you were in uniform for a while, too.

Mr. JACOBSON. I did. I enlisted in the United States Army Reserve from 1993 through 2001 with service in Bosnia. I then took a U.S. Navy commission as an intelligence officer and continue to serve in the Navy Reserve today.

Mr. VARGAS. Okay, thank you. I thought so. I wasn't sure about it, so I just wanted to make sure. So, I want to thank you also for your service, thank you.

Mr. JACOBSON. You're welcome, Congressman.

Mr. VARGAS. Thank you. Obviously, the issue here is the principle, I think, of do we exchange, do we negotiate, do we leave people behind? And, obviously, I mean, we've read a lot about what us politicians say, and I won't take the time to read it. I was going to read from the Congressional Record because it's interesting what politicians say when it's beneficial to them. There's lots of interesting things being said both sides.

I'd like to know what the military thinks about this, Mr. Waltz. You seem to have a good ear to what the Joint Chiefs of Staff and others are saying. What do they say about this deal? Are they criticizing it? Are they in favor of it, have they been critical of it? Do you know what the Joint Chiefs have said, or what they believe?

Mr. WALTZ. Congressman, you know, obviously many of our—we have civilian oversight of the military and our most senior leaders are supportive of this policy. I can tell you from the rank and file, anecdotally, that are reaching out to me, they're just as furious and resentful as we were at the time. And I think if things had been handled a little bit differently, if there had been a quiet reunion with the family and Sergeant Bergdahl had——immediately there hadn't been a rush to judgment to call him a hero, and tell the world he served with distinction you would have seen a very—a much more muted reaction.

Mr. VARGAS. So, it's not necessarily the principle of getting them back. You know, I was very curious when I listened to you and you said that, I believe, and I don't want to put words in your mouth, but I believe you said something we were out there looking for him and we were trying—and we should have, although we resented it, we were doing it. I mean, it sounded like you were doing what you thought you should have done.

Mr. WALTZ. That's right. I don't know of many folks who debate the principle that we should get every American back. I think what's debated and what's controversial is, one, his treatment when it was announced. But then, two, the price we paid. And I personally believe the price was too high. Some people draw the line at Khalid Sheik Mohammad. I draw the line in the top five senior Taliban members that were requested by the Taliban.

Mr. VARGAS. Thank you, sir. Dr. Jacobson, I'm going to ask you the same question, again. Thank you, sir, for your testimony. What about that notion, do you know where the Joints Chiefs of Staff, where are they on this? Are they against it, are the military in favor of it? If they are, why? Would you comment on that?

Mr. JACOBSON. I can only refer back in terms of the serving military leadership to the public statements made by Chairman of the Joint Staff Dempsey, General Odierno, and others. But two of my personal heroes who have retired from the military, General Jim Mattis and General Stanley McChrystal have been unequivocal in their support for that concept, and I'd be proud to stand where they are in this.

I do understand that some feel that it's the right thing to do, but they don't have to like it. There are a lot of missions in the military that soldiers, sailors, airmen, marines are very happy to do, that's why they're professionals, and they don't like it.

At the same time, I think what makes our nation so great is that I've spoken to many individuals who actually are very content with this, and didn't have a problem doing it. But I would find it strange if there was any less disagreement over the—how much one enjoyed having to do this, or whether or not we should have done it.

I'd be very surprised if there was that disagreement in the military.

Mr. VARGAS. Well, you know, I have to say one of the things that I find odd right here is it seems like no one is disagreeing with the principle that we should get this guy, it was just how it was handled, how it was handled, you know, saying that he was a hero, you know, giving the Rose Garden deal and all that. It doesn't seem like the principle is one that Mr. Waltz or—correct me if I'm wrong. It sounds like the principle is one you agree with. And I apologize——

Mr. WALTZ. Congressman, it's the principle and the price that we paid, and I would argue that we'll have to pay again to deal with these gentlemen in the future.

Mr. JACOBSON. And, Congressman, I think that it was a good price. I think this was worth the risk to get Sergeant Bergdahl back home.

Mr. VARGAS. Thank you, Mr. Chairman.

Mr. POE. The gentleman yields back. The Chair recognizes the gentleman from Florida, Mr. DeSantis, 5 minutes.

Mr. DESANTIS. Thank you, Mr. Chairman.

Mr. Jacobson, you had taken issue with Mr. Waltz when he had mentioned, I think correctly, that Mullah Omar thought this was a great thing for the liban. You said well, yes, maybe thought beheading Bergdahl would have been better for them. We can't say that. Do you honestly think if they thought beheading Bergdahl would have helped them that they would not have done it in a second? They did this, they got those men back because they want those guys back in command. Of course it was better for them, so I thought—that comment I thought was just—struck me as totally off base.

Let me ask you this, do we have troops in Afghanistan right now?

Mr. JACOBSON. Yes, Congressman.

Mr. DESANTIS. Okay. So, you have referenced troops who have been left behind. And we can argue whether Bergdahl left his unit behind. And I agree with Specialist Full, I think he did that, everyone that served with him said that. If we still have troops there, who have we left behind? We're still fighting the conflict. It's not over yet, so the notion that somehow had we not done this trade that means we "left him behind" is utter nonsense. So, what we've done is we've replenished the enemy in wartime when we still have fighters in there, and those individuals will be back on the battlefield, even if you believe this Qatar year. They're going to be back while we still under the President's timetable still have troops there. So, we have not left anybody behind.

And I think Mr. Waltz hits it right on the head about the price that you pay. Does this help or harm the security interest of the United States? I would refer to people, like to my colleague, Sam Johnson, who was a Medal of Honor winner, one of the most respected men in this body, prisoner of war. He said, "Absolutely not, this should not have been done." And when he was a prisoner of war, he would not have wanted to go back if it meant harming the security interest of his country. And when I talk to veterans in my district, and I have people who were POWs, they say the same thing. Yes, of course, we want to get everyone behind. We don't harm the country and put everyone else at risk to do that.

Mr. Andrews, did your son, Darryn, get honored at the White House for his service?

Mr. ANDREWS. No, sir.

Mr. DESANTIS. And you were never invited to any type of Rose Garden ceremony?

Mr. ANDREWS. No, sir.

Mr. DESANTIS. And I think a lot of veterans had a visceral reaction when they saw Bergdahl's parents given the lack of honorable service——

Mr. ANDREWS. That's when the people are calling me.

Mr. DESANTIS [continuing]. It was done to try to say we got a hero back. Susan Rice, honor and distinction, in order to divert the public's attention from the price that we paid. They didn't want the public focusing on the Taliban Five. They wanted the public focusing on we brought a soldier home, and so they had to inflate his service in order to try do that. So, it was an attempt at a deception of the public, and I think it struck a lot—I mean, me as a veteran and a lot of my folks in my district were very, very upset about that.

Let me ask you this. The Army lied to you, basically, about how your son died. Correct?

Mr. ANDREWS. They at least, at the very best didn't tell the whole story.

Mr. DESANTIS. Okay. So, knowing that, knowing that you didn't get the whole story, do you have confidence with this Bergdahl matter, we heard oh, we've got to let the military decide, but do you have confidence that they're going to do an investigation that's impartial and adequate?

Mr. ANDREWS. My personal feeling is if they will let the military do it and leave the politics out of it, I think they will do it.

Mr. DESANTIS. Do you think that if there is a high-ranking flag or general officer who's career could be impacted by how that case goes——

Mr. ANDREWS. See, that's putting politics back in.

Mr. DESANTIS. Well, I think, unfortunately, once you get up to that level, if that's where it is, and I'm a former JAG Prosecutor, so I'm worried about how it's working out.

Specialist Full, do you think that Mr. Bergdahl deserves an honorable discharge from the Army?

Mr. FULL. No, I do not. It's a slap in the face to all those that did serve honorably, upheld their oath, and didn't desert, that he gets the same benefits that they do.

Mr. DESANTIS. And if he goes—if this case gets diverted for whatever way and he's not actually found guilty at a court-martial and given a punitive discharge, is it your understanding that he would then be entitled to back pay for all the years that he was gone?

Mr. FULL. Yes, he would be entitled to back pay, which I think is around $300,000, college benefits, VA health care benefits, everything a veteran gets with an honorable discharge.

Mr. DESANTIS. So, you think that given what happened, you know, if you were advising a prosecutor as to what to ask for the penalty, would a dishonorable discharge be one of the things that they should ask the military judge or the members for?

Mr. FULL. Yes, reduced in rank, forfeiture of all pay, and a dishonorable discharge is what I'd recommend.

Mr. DESANTIS. Well, I appreciate that. I am concerned—I mean, I have been involved in the Military Justice System. There is an inherent amount of lot of politics involved when you get at that level, and I think it's important that this is transparent. And I think Congress needs to conduct oversight. You know, how Nidal Hasan was handled, to me, was a travesty that it took that long, and he got over $300,000 just sitting in the brig. So, I appreciate the witnesses, and I yield back.

Mr. POE. The gentleman yields back. The Chair will recognize the gentle lady from Florida, Ms. Frankel, for 5 minutes.

Ms. FRANKEL. Thank you, Mr. Poe. Again, I want to just, to Mr. and Mrs. Andrews, I just—my heart breaks for you. I'm so sorry, I'm sorry that you have to be here. And I'll try not to politicize this really for your benefit. To the other gentlemen really thank you, again, for your service. I cannot tell you how much as a mother of—and I don't want to keep hoisting my son up, but I understand your bravery, your selflessness, just thank you, thank you, thank you.

My first question is to Dr. Jacobson, and if the others want to answer, fine. What can we learn from Sergeant Bergdahl? I know we're bringing him back, we've been talking in all types of disparaging ways about him. We don't know that much about him, at least I don't. But what can we learn from his capture? Can he give us valuable information?

Mr. JACOBSON. Absolutely, Congresswoman Frankel. I know Representative Kinzinger knows from his time going through SERE training, a lot of what we understand now about captivity, a lot of what can do to help innoculate our personnel against those stresses comes from, unfortunately, the experience of individuals who were held captive not just during our wars, but during peacetime detention. So, as we have heard from the military, there is going to be a debriefing process, and in that one can hope that there is information that one day might save the life or make it less problematic for future U.S. personnel who are held in captivity in the inevitable conflicts in the future.

Ms. FRANKEL. I believe for—without debating the merits of how long we stayed in Afghanistan, I do believe that we were there because our own freedoms were jeopardized by al-Qaeda, and they were being protected by the Taliban. I want to talk about those freedoms.

What sets us apart from the Taliban? Specifically, I know you probably all agree, you go to fight for our freedom, freedom of speech, freedom of religion, and there's something else I would respectfully like to suggest, which is our due process of law that we have in this country, and what a high standard it is. So, my question to all of you is should soldiers who misbehave be subject to due process of law?

Mr. FULL. Well, he's a member of the armed forces. He's not subject to a civilian or Federal court, he's subject to UCMJ action.

Ms. FRANKEL. Should he have due process even though it's a military court?

Mr. FULL. Yes, that's the whole point that I'm coming forward and telling my side of the story. He deserted, he's back, great he's back, but he needs to face and be held accountable for his actions.

Ms. FRANKEL. Yes, Mr. Waltz?

Mr. WALTZ. Congresswoman, there was a real fear, me included in those first 24 hours that there would be, you know, "ticker tape parades," and Rose Garden ceremonies, and that this whole effort would get politicized, and that the truth, frankly, would be buried. And that's why both myself, Specialist Full, and others have come forward.

Ms. FRANKEL. Okay. So, I think we agree, though, the due process of law, that he's entitled to that.

Mr. FULL. Absolutely.

Ms. FRANKEL. And, lastly, I mean, I want to—anyone who wants to answer this question. This I'm coming at as a mother, all right? Which is, do you believe all our soldiers, all these men and women who go into battle, go into war are perfect? Do we bring in perfect people?

Mr. JACOBSON. I hope my friend Mike will agree. When you've been in charge of junior troops, hardly a day probably goes by, it's almost like being a parent, where a parent—kids are imperfect. I'm sure my mother would say the same thing, but that's why it's so important to have well trained NCOs, to have good leaders in those positions to guide these troops through something that's unbelievably stressful, and to ensure that they all get home alive.

Ms. FRANKEL. Well, I do know this. I don't know very much about Mr. Bergdahl or his family, or what he was going through, what his mom was going through. I hope that will be determined as you have suggested. I think that's fair. But I do know this, that so many of our young men and women are coming home and they have been stressed out, and are mentally unstable. And I would not like to think that they would not be subject to due process if they committed a crime.

So, with that, I want to thank you, thank you all of you for your service. Again, Mr. and Mrs. Andrews, really I'm so sorry for your loss. And, Mr. Chair, I yield the rest of my time.

Mr. POE. The gentle lady yields back. And just so the record is clear, Mr. Andrews served in the United States Air Force, so all four of you all, thank you for your service.

Ms. FRANKEL. Thank you for your service, sir.

Mr. POE. The Chair recognizes the gentleman from Florida, Mr. Yoho, for 5 minutes.

Mr. YOHO. Thank you, Mr. Chairman, panelists. I appreciate your being here, and thank you for your service to our great country.

Mr. and Mrs. Andrews, thank you for the sacrifice of what you went through. I, as a grateful citizen of this great nation and a Member of Congress am appreciative every day of the liberties and freedoms that we get to experience because of the willingness of people to serve, commit, and dedicate to this country. I thank you.

I think we should keep the narrative on the policy. The description of whether or not he was a deserter or not, as you brought up,

Specialist Full, that will come out and it will go through its due process.

Mr. Waltz, you said in your bio, you state that you deal or provide strategic analysis and policy development for other countries. Was the transfer of one American soldier for five Taliban a wise decision in your opinion?

Mr. WALTZ. Congressman, I think we should look at this policy as a whole and learn from it. Right now, a gentleman by the name of Mullah Abdul Zakir is the head of the Taliban Military Committee that we released previously from Guantanamo, and we're paying that price now. And further, Abu Bakr al-Baghdadi, head of ISIS that's terrorizing Syria and Iraq right now, was also detained in Camp Bucca. We need to learn lessons from these releases that we're paying for later.

Mr. YOHO. So, in your opinion it's probably not a wise policy to implement.

Mr. Jacobson, you and Mr. Sherman were referring to our democracy, and you brought in Israel, as democracies trade for prisoners all the time. And I know I don't need to remind you, but this is not Israel, we're not Israel. We don't do that as a policy. And you're talking about a democracy, and again I know I don't have to remind you, a true democracy is majority rule, it's mob rule. And what I hear the public want to do with Mr. Bergdahl is mob rule. And I had to remind people we're a constitutional republic where the minority is protected by rule of law. And as Ben Franklin always talked about, a democracy is two wolves and a sheep deciding what to have for lunch. That sheep always loses, and so I'm thankful that we're in a republic. And we need to remind people that we are different because we do follow that.

And as far as Mr. Bergdahl, he will come home. And I think any time we get an American soldier back to our country we all should celebrate. But I think before we hang judgment on him, was he wrong or right, we need to look at and let the military go through what they're going to go through to decide the fate of that young man.

The issues that I want to ask you about, do we negotiate with terrorists or not? And, again, I think Specialist Full, you brought up they're terrorist. It's not even a nation, it's a terrorist group. And, again, this goes against our precedents, it goes against our historical policy. Do you think this is a wise thing that we do, or implement?

Mr. JACOBSON. Congressman, I certainly think that it's a wise thing that we retrieved Sergeant Bergdahl.

Mr. YOHO. There's no doubt about that, but negotiate with terrorists.

Mr. JACOBSON. I want to run through just a list of a couple of situations where we have negotiated not only with terrorists, but with insurgent groups, and state-sponsors of terrorism. As I mentioned, part of bringing the war in Afghanistan to conclusion will be continuing discussions with the Taliban, but taking a look back at our own history, not just discussions that we've had with the North Koreans. We also——

Mr. YOHO. Okay, North Korea, that's a country, it's not a terror——

Mr. JACOBSON. They sponsor terrorism.

Mr. YOHO. They're a country.

Mr. JACOBSON. Was a state-sponsor of terrorism.

Mr. YOHO. Okay.

Mr. JACOBSON. I also look back, as I said, if you understand that there are differences between insurgents, between terrorists, between state-sponsors of terrorism, the concern I think people have is this idea of ransom for a hostage. And I look back even at what—and I'm going to give you allied and U.S. examples: Ronald Reagan in terms of what happened with the Arms for Hostages deal. Margaret Thatcher and her secret talks with the IRA. No one would discount that the IRA was terrorist group.

Sometimes you end up sitting across the table from those who have the blood of your friends on their hands to bring peace. And if that is the case that we are seeing, if that's what sitting down with the Taliban means, then I fully support that.

Mr. YOHO. Okay. Let me ask you both, Mr. Waltz and Dr. Jacobson, did the President by not consulting with Congress 30 days before in your opinion break the law? Mr. Waltz?

Mr. WALTZ. Congressman, that's my understanding of the law. I'm not a legal expert, but my understanding of the law was that Congress was to be consulted.

Mr. YOHO. Dr. Jacobson?

Mr. JACOBSON. I'm not a lawyer, and you're all going to argue about that statute, but I think what the President did, acting on short notice was absolutely the right thing to do.

Mr. YOHO. I yield back. Thank you.

Mr. POE. The gentleman yields back his time. The Chair recognizes the gentleman from Texas, Mr. Castro, for 5 minutes.

Mr. CASTRO. Thank you, Mr. Chairman. And to Mr. and Mrs. Andrews, my condolences and safe travels on your way back to Texas. I represent San Antonio. Thank you for being here, and thank you all, all your gentlemen for your service.

And I agree with part of Mr. Yoho's statement that I want to focus on the policy, the agreement that was made for Sergeant Bergdahl and that transfer has been made. There's still a debate going on about whether that was good or bad, but I think the most constructive thing that we can get out of this hearing is what we do in the future.

And in that vein, I think there's two issues here. First, if someone deserts their unit, should we go retrieve that person? And then second, what is the appropriate deal that we should make for a soldier? So, it sounds like, at least, the prevailing idea is that even if somebody deserts, we should still try to retrieve that person. Does anybody on the panel differ or disagree with that principle?

Mr. WALTZ. Congressman, I think it comes down to a matter of intent. Dr. Jacobson raised the issue in the case of Mr. Jenkins who deserted into North Korea. To my knowledge, there were no attempts to bring him home until he appeared 40 years later in Japan.

Mr. CASTRO. But would you, and I know that it has not been adjudicated whether he deserted or not. I know that there is some evidence within—among the other soldiers that suggests that perhaps he did, but that has not been adjudicated. But assuming for

66

the sake of argument that he did, does that mean that if somebody deserts that we shouldn't go get him? Should we change policy next time?

Mr. FULL. Well, I think the problem as has been stated is they brought him to a hero's welcome, and we're not the only people that knew that he walked off on his own accord. There was an original investigation done.

Mr. CASTRO. Sure.

Mr. FULL. It's still open because they have to get his side of the story, but everybody knew that he walked off on his own.

Mr. CASTRO. So, assuming that he did this, right, and that there's no argument, then you're saying still bring him home, just don't celebrate it. That would be your point.

Mr. FULL. Why would you call him a hero when there's people like his son who pushed somebody down and took an RPG round.

Mr. CASTRO. Right.

Mr. FULL. And gave his life for another one who is a hero, that didn't get a hero's welcome.

Mr. CASTRO. But in terms of the policy, you would still say go get that person.

Mr. FULL. I don't know. I'm not—I'm truthful.

Mr. CASTRO. And then to my second question, what is the appropriated deal that we should make to have a soldier return. Right? There is a big issue here over whether you negotiate with terrorists, or only nation states, but I think that the difficulty we're running into here is that our enemies in this common era are no longer just nation states. They are groups like al-Qaeda, Haqqani Network, and others.

So, let me ask you, Mr. Waltz, because you were both a soldier and you're a policy expert. What deal would you have made for Sergeant Bergdahl?

Mr. WALTZ. Congressman, my own view is in any negotiation both sides should walk away unhappy. That means it's about right. And in this case the enemy walked away happy. The enemy walked away declaring victory, and received exactly what they asked for. I don't think that was good negotiation on our part.

Mr. CASTRO. But how does that translate—what would you have given—if you were writing policy, what would you have exchanged for Sergeant Bergdahl?

Mr. WALTZ. Congressman, there's a number of lower-level detainees held in Afghanistan and other places. I think it was the—a lot has been mentioned about trading numbers. The issue for me here is the quality.

Mr. CASTRO. So, you might have given 100 people for one person if they were lower level folks.

Mr. WALTZ. I don't like it. I think that's a policy issue that had to be debated, but the decision that was made, these five, was a bad decision.

Mr. CASTRO. Did we get anything in exchange, Mr. Jacobson, did we get anything in exchange for the prisoners that were released from GITMO by President Bush?

Mr. JACOBSON. Not that I'm aware of, but I have to say the news reports I can remember from that time period, there was talk about political deals and that, but I—nothing like the Bergdahl situation.

Mr. CASTRO. So, that was just a straight release, essentially, of those folks?

Mr. JACOBSON. Yes.

Mr. CASTRO. Okay. Chairman, I yield back my time.

Mr. POE. Thank the gentleman from Texas. The Chair recognizes another gentleman from Texas, Mr. Weber, 5 minutes.

Mr. WEBER. Thank you. Specialist Full, what would you say is the—was the morale in your unit following this illegal prisoner exchange?

Mr. FULL. I'm not in the Army any more, sir.

Mr. WEBER. Would you hazard a guess?

Mr. FULL. Oh, as far as us when we're talking?

Mr. WEBER. Absolutely.

Mr. FULL. Well, we were very upset with it. Like I said numerous times, with the hero's welcome.

Mr. WEBER. Okay. In your opinion, would this have set up this agreement between an enlisted officer and those rank and file soldiers, or were they pretty much in agreement this was a bad deal?

Mr. FULL. This is a bad deal all around.

Mr. WEBER. All the way around.

Mr. FULL. Nobody in the Blackfoot Company that would——

Mr. WEBER. If you could say anything to President Obama regarding this trade, what would you say?

Mr. FULL. I'm not going to say that.

Mr. WEBER. Fair enough. Mr. Waltz, you're forewarned, same questions. What would you say would be the morale of those units following this prisoner exchange?

Mr. WALTZ. Fairly low, Congressman. And in terms of your second question, I would point the President to the heroes at the end of this table.

Mr. WEBER. Okay.

Mr. WALTZ. They deserve the same level of treatment.

Mr. WEBER. Would you advise him to make the same trade twice?

Mr. WALTZ. No, Congressman, I wouldn't. And just a follow-on to the previous Congressman's question. I think there are a lot of other policy options open that weren't fully explored, more pressure on Pakistan, for one. He was held by the Haqqani Network which has been described as a veritable arm of the Pakistani Intelligence Service. There are a number of other options that were on the table besides a trade.

Mr. WEBER. Okay. Dr. Jacobson, what would you say to the President?

Mr. JACOBSON. Congressman, I would say good job, absolutely go do this again, bring our soldier home.

Mr. WEBER. Mr. Andrews, after having sat here, and thank you very much, and you, Mrs. Andrews for being here, after sitting through this hearing, what now would you say to this committee?

Mr. ANDREWS. For one thing, 5 minutes isn't as long as it used to be, but what I would say to the committee is my son was a soldier's soldier, and it didn't matter what the assignment was, he was going to do it. And I don't believe that you have to be a perfect person to follow the Military Code of Justice. You have a book right there. Read the book and do what it says. It's not that complicated.

But do not let my son—to me, this situation with us not being told the whole truth, and then trading a private for five high-ranking Taliban, exactly why did my son die? Tell me one more time, because I don't know what we've accomplished.

Mr. WEBER. If you could say that to the President, is that what you would say to him?

Mr. ANDREWS. Yes.

Mr. WEBER. And now the hard questions, and forgive me. If you could get your son back by trading five more of those senior Taliban?

Mr. ANDREWS. If my son had been a deserter, then no, absolutely not. But my son was a man of honor, and I would do almost anything.

Mr. WEBER. Thank you, folks. Mr. Chairman, I yield back.

Mr. POE. The gentleman yields back his time. The Chair recognizes the gentleman from Pennsylvania, Mr. Perry, 5 minutes.

Mr. PERRY. Thank you, Mr. Chairman. I want to thank each of you gentlemen for your service. Certainly, Mr. Andrews, I want to let you know as someone who's worn the uniform that many Americans feel like the actions by the administration and the President have diminished your son's service, and your and his sacrifice. And I let you know that I'm of that opinion, but I also want to let you know that he has done a great thing for the men that he served with, and the ones that are particularly alive because of his actions, and a very grateful nation. So, I just want to thank you for your sacrifice, as well.

Turn to questions. I'll start with Mr. Jacobson. You keep saying, or at least I've heard you say a couple of times the end of the war regarding the reference of prisoner swaps. And I'm just wondering has the Taliban, as far as you know, stated that they consider the war to be coming to a close?

Mr. JACOBSON. Congressman, I was referring to the end of conflict in the Second World War and Korean, specifically.

Mr. PERRY. So, the paradigm is not the same, is my point. We might be drawing down, but the Taliban, as far as you know, are they going to continue to fight?

Mr. JACOBSON. Well, the Taliban have been in talks with the United States for several years.

Mr. PERRY. As far as you know, do we have any reason to believe right now they're not going to continue to fight when we stop?

Mr. JACOBSON. I don't believe we are stopping the fight, Congressman.

Mr. PERRY. We're just in disengagement. Right? So, the war is still going to continue as far as you know.

Mr. JACOBSON. We're still working with the Afghans not only to try——

Mr. PERRY. All right. I got it. I got it. So, are you—when you say that these folks that we released have been so long gone from the battlefield that they can't be relevant, are you aware that Mr. Baghdadi, who's currently running ISIS, was released in 2005? This is now 2014. Is he still relevant on the battlefield today?

Mr. JACOBSON. I can't comment to a specific situation. I'm not——

Mr. PERRY. I can comment. He's damn relevant, sir. Let me move on.

Mr. Full, there was an investigation regarding Mr. Bergdahl's absence conducted at some point. Right? And I imagine you gave sworn statements in that regard?

Mr. FULL. Yes, 15–6.

Mr. PERRY. Right. So, do you think that the Army is aware of the circumstances, his circumstances of departure?

Mr. FULL. Yes.

Mr. PERRY. You do. And I do, as well. I would like to turn to Mr. Waltz at this point.

Understanding your circumstances if captured, what is your understanding if you were captured on the battlefield of what we would do, and what we wouldn't do, what you could expect from your country?

Mr. WALTZ. Congressman, we deploy knowing the high likelihood of being captured, and it comes with that understanding that ransoms will not be paid, and there will not be swaps for us. The United States will do everything it can to get us back, but there's limits to what the country is going to do. And I personally would not want anything done that's going to harm our ongoing national security or endanger my fellow soldiers.

Mr. PERRY. Were you ever given the impression when you took the oath, or any time after that, that the United States would jeopardize our national security on your behalf to get you out of——

Mr. FULL. Absolutely not, Congressman, nor would I want that to happen.

Mr. PERRY. So, let me ask you, you're a Special Operator. On June 3rd, the AP reported that the United States Government knew the whereabouts of Mr. Bergdahl from three sources, UAS, satellite, and human intelligence. You're a special operator and you know the capability—you got out in 2009. Right? It's now 2014, things have changed a little bit, but I know you stay involved and in touch with your community.

My point is the options. Right? So, we had some options on the table and we chose to trade five high-value targets for one service member, right, that we wanted to free and have come back home, which is laudable to have him come back home. It is the right thing to do.

Do you have any lack of confidence in your ability, of your unit, the United States Army with the capabilities we have, if we knew where he was, your ability if tasked with the mission and given the resources to go and retrieve that soldier?

Mr. WALTZ. I don't know the details of——

Mr. PERRY. I know you don't.

Mr. WALTZ. But if we knew where he was and we were confident, and the risks were evaluated, absolutely we have the capability to get him.

Mr. PERRY. So, you already spoke about the different options that we had or didn't have, and you don't think this was the best one. If we knew where he was, can you think—can you come up with some scenario where we have people on the ground that do what you did for a living, that we wouldn't exercise that option?

Mr. WALTZ. The only scenario that comes to mind, sir, is that this was part of a broader policy initiative to open up talks with the Taliban; that this was a confidence-building measure, and this has been discussed for some time now, that potentially this trade would be a confidence-building measure as a first step toward future talks. That's the only plausible scenario that I can come up with.

Mr. PERRY. My time is expired, I yield back. Thank you.

Mr. POE. The gentleman yields back his time. The Chair recognizes the gentleman from Wisconsin, Mr. Duffy, for 5 minutes.

Mr. DUFFY. Thank you, Mr. Chairman.

First of all, to respond to my colleague across the aisle about due process, all of us agree on due process. The conversation happening today is not about due process, the conversation today is about the decision the administration made for the five Taliban members in exchange for Sergeant Bergdahl. That's the conversation. We all believe in due process. We're Americans.

Mr. Waltz, I think it was you who indicated that you had conversation about your country will never leave you behind. And I don't know if it was you or Specialist Full who had mentioned you thought it was that your country won't leave any honorable man behind. Specialist Full, was that your comment?

Mr. FULL. Yes, it was.

Mr. DUFFY. Was Sergeant Bergdahl left behind?

Mr. FULL. No.

Mr. DUFFY. No.

Mr. FULL. He walked off on his own.

Mr. DUFFY. He left. Correct?

Mr. FULL. Yes, he left.

Mr. DUFFY. So, he wasn't left behind. He walked off.

Mr. FULL. He left us behind.

Mr. DUFFY. Right. And, Dr. Jacobson, you've indicated that the fight is not over. Right? They're going to continue this fight. It's not over, peace has not been declared with the Taliban.

Mr. JACOBSON. That's correct, Congressman.

Mr. DUFFY. So, with the war or the fight that's going to continue, it seems to me the argument that well, we're all putting our arms down, and the conflict is going to end. This exchange makes sense. That's what we do. World War II when the war is over, we put down our arms, we exchange our prisoners and everyone is happy. But that's not this case, right?

Mr. JACOBSON. Well, that's not——

Mr. DUFFY. This case you've said the fight will continue, and with the fight still going on, we took someone who allegedly walked away from his post in exchange for five high-level Taliban members, and the fight continues. Am I wrong on this?

Mr. JACOBSON. The fight continued in Korea after the prisoner exchanges, the fight continued in World War II after the exchanges in 1944, the fight will continue in Afghanistan. My argument is that the risk of putting these five individuals on the battlefield is mitigated by a number of factors to include all the accomplishments that we've seen in Afghanistan over the past several years.

Mr. DUFFY. I'll get to the risk in a second, but in regard to the prior swaps that have been made, those swaps have been made with nation states. Correct? Do you have an example where we've had swaps with a non-nation state before this one?

Mr. JACOBSON. The examples I have, and you term this a swap. The examples I have of negotiation with non-nation——

Mr. DUFFY. I didn't ask—I'm talking a swap, we exchange prisoners with a non-nation state, or better yet for a deserter, if that's what he—the military finds him to be.

Mr. JACOBSON. The closest thing I can think of is after the Battle of Mogadishu and the negotiations to get back Chief Warrant Officer Michael Durant.

Mr. DUFFY. But not with—you don't have a prior example of a swap with a non-nation state. This is——

Mr. JACOBSON. Well, that was with Mohammed Farrah Aidid who was not a nation state.

Mr. DUFFY. In regard to the threat that this now poses, Mr. and Mrs. Andrews talk about a son, and how he may—that he would be able to make that exchange to bring his own son back. I think every heart breaks in here thinking about what his family has gone through and the sacrifice that his son made for his country.

Do you feel pretty comfortable that with these five Taliban members released that we won't have another hearing like this of another American family who lost a son or daughter who's over fighting on behalf of the country because of these five that were released, or do you feel pretty comfortable that America is a safer place, and our men and women are safer in those foreign lands?

Mr. JACOBSON. Our men and women who put on the uniform are always at risk regardless of what happened or will happen.

Mr. DUFFY. That's not my question. I'm talking about the five that were released.

Mr. JACOBSON. I'm comfortable with the judgment that was made by our military leaders that all the risks involved, the risk of potentially these individuals ending back up on the battlefield, the risks of not getting Bergdahl. I'm comfortable that the assessment they made and the recommendations they made are the right one.

Mr. DUFFY. Mr. Waltz, I think you said the Taliban got their top five draft picks in exchange for Sergeant Bergdahl.

Mr. WALTZ. Yes, sir.

Mr. DUFFY. Good trade?

Mr. WALTZ. Absolutely not.

Mr. POE. The gentleman from Wisconsin yields back his time. The gentleman from California, Mr. Rohrabacher, is recognized for 5 minutes.

Mr. ROHRABACHER. Thank you very much, Mr. Chairman. I've been running in and out of meetings like everybody else here. We're overwhelmed, so I'm sorry if I cover any territory that's already been covered here.

Let me just note that I disagree with the statement that our policy has been to do everything we can to get back a prisoner. That is not the case, that is not policy for our Government. Everything we can? No, even the people who are in the field totally understand that we're not going to do things that will further put other Americans at severe risk in order to get them back. They understand that. And that's part of why they're heroes, and that's part of the reason Mr. Andrews' son is a hero. He knew he was taking a chance, and that even if he was captured that we would not be doing things that would put the American people at risk to get him back home. So, I want to make sure that is a very significant point for people to understand in the discussion of this.

Second of all, I'd like to point out that there are other alternatives to try to get these guys back, or man back, Mr. Bergdahl, than just giving up these five leaders of the Taliban. We could have, for example—I have seen no evidence. Mr. Jacobson, have you see any evidence that there was pressure put on Pakistan in order to get the Taliban to return this prisoner?

Mr. JACOBSON. Congressman Rohrabacher, I'm not aware of the specifics of those negotiations. I've only seen——

Mr. ROHRABACHER. All right. So, you're unaware of the—you're unaware, I'm unaware. I've been looking, there is no indication here that this administration didn't even put pressure on the major supporter, the ISI in Pakistan to do what they could do to get back this prisoner. Instead, they gave up five murderous leaders. Let's take a look at who they are. We know that one of them was perhaps engaged in the strategizing for 9/11, which resulted in 3,000 Americans being slaughtered in front of our face. He's being let go. Then there is Mullah Mohammad Fazl, I guess that's how you pronounce his name. I know about this man. I know that a long time ago he was, in fact, captured. This is, you might say, a second time he was released, you might say, because he was captured early on in 2001 after 9/11, and he was put into a French Fort with hundreds of other Taliban leaders and Taliban fighters, and there is a tradition in Afghanistan. The tradition is it's almost the law that the people live by, it is their core principles as Afghans, and that is once you are captured you do not try to overpower the person who has captured you. And the reason that they have that as part of their law is because over the centuries they would have had to kill all of their prisoners if they didn't uphold that. So, as part of their honor as a person to not—once you're captured, you do not try to overcome your captors.

Well, what happened in this case with Mr. Fazl? Yes, I'm sure that he's already promised us that he wouldn't go back to doing something and causing—putting our people at risk, or attacking Americans, but at that time he led an uprising against his captors. They murdered about 50 Afghans where General Dostum's Afghani wife introduced Chairman Poe to General Dostum before. And they murdered his—the guys who were holding them captive, but they also murdered a CIA officer named Mike Spann.

I visited that spot, I visited the spot where Mike Spann had been murdered shortly after he was murdered, and this is the guy that are one of the five guys we are releasing. We're releasing a man who's already murdered the first real American to lose his life in the Afghan War, we're releasing him now.

You think that's going to maybe indicate that we're strong? Does this release indicate that we are strong, and that we are people—that they're going to have to deal with the United States of America in terms of our military strength? No, they're going to deal with people who they think are weak, and are cowards, and they will be willing then to kill more Americans, and to capture more Americans in order to cut more deals.

This is a travesty. The President of the United States has maybe got himself into a position here that I don't know if maybe he thinks of himself as a peacemaker. I think this will, in the end, have just the opposite impact, and I think a rational discussion will do that.

Mr. Chairman, I've got 6 seconds, and I actually would like to give our witness the chance to retort to that.

Mr. POE. Quickly.

Mr. JACOBSON. Respectfully, I disagree, Congressman.

Mr. ROHRABACHER. Fine, yes. That's it? Okay. Thank you very much.

Mr. JACOBSON. If the chairman—at the chairman's pleasure I'm happy to continue. I was being succint.

Mr. POE. No, time has expired.

Mr. ROHRABACHER. All right. Thank you very much.

Mr. POE. Thank you, though. The Chair recognizes the gentleman from Georgia, Mr. Collins, for 5 minutes.

Mr. COLLINS. Thank you, Mr. Chairman, I apologize. This is one of the days when everything goes long. Again, I'm Air Force Reserve, I am the chaplain, I served in Iraq. Having been on the unfortunate end of the door that you opened, and understand this all too well.

The issues that come up for me, and some of this may be a little bit of follow-up on my colleague who just mentioned—but, Mr. Jacobson, I have a question. You keep bringing up, or you brought up before the fact that they're not going back to the same Afghanistan that they left, and that they would not have the probable impact that they could have had. What leads you—what intelligence, what information, what would have you to believe that they couldn't get spun up pretty quickly in a country that's not changed a whole lot in 4-, 5-, 6-, 700 years? I mean, what would cause you to believe that?

Mr. JACOBSON. Congressman, in my experience in Afghanistan, again both as an intelligence officer, and then later on as a civilian advisor where I worked with senior Afghan officials every day, I do believe there have been a great number of changes if just in the last decade alone.

For example, I believe that most of the networks that these individuals had when they were a force fighting against the Northern Alliance no longer exist. Many of their friends are dead, many of the Taliban leadership are dead. And I also believe that the Afghan people have changed.

You have seen just in the recent elections, this open defiance of threats to kill people who would go vote, 40 percent of the voters, I believe, were women who were told do not do this.

Mr. COLLINS. Let me stop you right there for a second. We saw a great deal of turnout in the Iraqi elections, too, and now we're looking at almost a breakdown to civil war. I mean, pointing to an election is a great thing, but also pointing to a change of hearts, minds, and attitudes, I'm not sure you're actually getting there. So, I mean, we just might probably, respectfully, just have a difference of opinion here.

I believe that they may not walk back into the same structure that they had before, but I do not believe it's going to take them very long to build from scratch or to bring in others that—there's a reason they were wanted them. There's a reason they wanted these five. I don't believe that they just picked out, said give us five, we'll give you him. And I think there's a reason for that.

The other situation that I would like maybe some general discussion about is something that keeps coming up here. Well, we're drawing down our action, we're drawing down this war. And it was—I don't know, Mr. Waltz, if it was you or someone else that basically talked about the fact that we're dealing with the Taliban. We're dealing with terrorist organizations in this global war on terrorism, not the global war on Afghanistan, not the global war on a country. And, granted, when we ended World War II there was country state versus country state. We had a—we're not in that situation any more, and I'm just curious to know is, when does the fact that we're fighting—and I don't believe the Taliban, or al-Qaeda, or any of these other terrorist networks have changed their opinion of the West. Do you believe they changed their opinion of the West, or they still have the desire to wreak havoc on the West?

Mr. JACOBSON. I actually believe our actions in Afghanistan have split views amongst the Taliban. I don't think there's a single unified view any more.

Mr. COLLINS. Interesting, but I think among the larger terrorist network as a whole, and we can go look at that, I think there is still a vast determination there, is we go forward. So, I'm not sure what—when we draw the line now with dealing with, negotiating with, however we want to do this. It just—Specialist, talk about this for a second.

Given the fact that we traded, and there's some who will give an argument that this was the end of the war. We had to do it, a political outcome at some point. But is this a price that you would ever have envisioned paying if—for someone who walked off or didn't walk off? Is this what we are sort of looking at? Not that we give up, but the price that we give up?

Mr. FULL. We're still at war with the Taliban whether people want to admit it or not. And just because we stop fighting them, doesn't mean that they're going to stop wanting to kill us, and fight us. No, when I signed an oath it was an understanding, as Mr. Waltz has said, that I knew there would be a certain price up to a point that the United States would pay to get me back. And if that was me over there, no, you could have left me over there. I would not have wanted you to trade five high-level Taliban operatives for myself.

Mr. COLLINS. Well, the curious for me at this point is, if five was the price this time, what's the price next time, the President stepping down, cabinet members stepping down, Congress giving them more money? What's the price, because we're not dealing with a nation state here. We're dealing with thugs, we're dealing with rogues, we're dealing with now the same ideological bent that is going through many of the Middle Eastern countries, and Iraq is simply a forum, what I'm fearful is going to Afghanistan.

I appreciate you being here. This is just very much of a concern for many folks because they do not understand why this happened the way it did, given the fact that most believe that this war is not over, and that we will see these guys again one way or the other.

Mr. Chairman, I yield back.

Mr. POE. The gentleman yields back. The Chair will recognize the ranking member for one additional question, and recognize itself for an additional question.

Mr. SHERMAN. Thank you. I'll note that in 1944 when we did a prisoner exchange it was with the Nazis. And, of course, that war continued for another year.

Mr. POE. Would the gentleman yield?

Mr. SHERMAN. Yes, I'll yield.

Mr. COLLINS. Would the gentleman also recognize that the Nazi Government at that time represented Germany as a nation state?

Mr. SHERMAN. Yes, but if you think——

Mr. COLLINS. Okay. But al-Qaeda never represented anyone as a nation state.

Mr. SHERMAN. Al-Qaeda did control and govern, with the acquiescence of the United States, the vast majority of Afghanistan until 9/11. But, more importantly, if you want to create groups that are anathema to the United States, I put the Nazis right at the top.

Mr. COLLINS. Well, I think they also——

Mr. SHERMAN. In any case, I have not yielded any further.

Mr. Jacobson, only an investigation is going to disclose the real facts behind Sergeant Bergdahl's disappearance and his capture, but we've heard substantial evidence that Sergeant Bergdahl acted in an inappropriate and inexplicable manner.

Can you describe the kinds of stresses that somebody, and Sergeant Bergdahl would have faced in Afghanistan, and whether that would cause someone, not everyone, but some to act in an inexplicable manner? I realize that the vast majority of our soldiers, Marines, et cetera, are subjected to those pressures and do not act inexplicably.

Mr. FULL. Can I have permission to speak?

Mr. SHERMAN. Yes.

Mr. FULL. Well, you're asking Dr. Jacobson what situation Bergdahl was in over there. I was with Bergdahl at the same location. I could give you a firsthand account of exactly what Bergdahl was going through because I went through the exact same conditions.

Mr. SHERMAN. Well, then I'll ask you then to respond to the question first, and then Dr. Jacobson to respond second. I was asking more in a general sphere as to what you face in Afghanistan but, obviously, you know the specifics.

Mr. FULL. We were at an observation post. It was very primitive, we had to eat Meals Ready to Eat which are heated up with water. It was very hot, very dirty, went without showers for certain days, didn't get phone calls or any comforts of home, but it didn't affect anybody else there. We all continued the mission and upheld our oath.

Everybody deals with mental issues in some form or another if they deploy to Afghanistan or Iraq. Everybody else still came back from that same platoon. Nobody else deserted on their own, so there's nothing in my opinion that was so bad that forced him to walk off on his own accord caused by anything going on over there. He walked off on his own accord.

Mr. SHERMAN. Dr. Jacobson, obviously, the vast majority of those in his unit were not affected to the point where they engaged in inappropriate behavior, and, obviously, anyone in Afghanistan is subject to being shelled, or subject to an IED at just about any time. Can you describe the pressures that people are under, and whether that could explain the inexplicable?

Mr. JACOBSON. Well, Congressman, I won't make a claim to be able to explain the unexplicable or inexplicable, but what I will say is that the stresses of combat are tremendous. From my own experience, which was not nearly as far forward in either deployment as either of my colleagues to the right, you still have fear, fear of being kidnapped, fear of being shot at, fear of being shelled, mortared, what have you. There is tremendous sleep deprivation for being on long combat patrols or being woken in the night to enemy action.

I do agree that you've raised perhaps one of the most important points, and that is that just because there is combat stress doesn't excuse actions such as walking away from one's post, but this is exactly why you have to have the full investigation to determine what happened, and why it happened in the hopes that we can prevent that from happening again, and hold those individuals who need to be held accountable, accountable in the Military Justice System.

Mr. SHERMAN. Thank you. And just to correct the record, I once said al-Qaeda when I meant to say the Taliban. I yield back.

Mr. POE. The Chair has one additional question for all four of you. The way I understand the law is that before people are released from Guantanamo Bay, prisoners there, that the Secretary of Defense must explain why it is in the national security interest of the United States to release that specific prisoner.

Assume that is the law, and from your point of view, what was the national security interest, or do you believe there was a national security interest of the United States in releasing those five individuals? Dr. Jacobson, do you believe there was a national security interest of the United States?

Mr. JACOBSON. Yes, I do, Congressman.

Mr. POE. Mr. Waltz?

Mr. WALTZ. Congressman, I believe America is less safe and the world is more dangerous with the release of those individuals.

Mr. POE. Sergeant Full?

Mr. FULL. I believe America is less safe, and the world is also in more danger.

Mr. POE. And, Mr. Andrews, I'll give you the last word.

Mr. ANDREWS. Thank you. I believe America is less safe. I believe these five guys are going to come after us. I believe that it was a mistake to release them, and that that did not serve our national interest in any way.

Mr. POE. I want to thank you all for being here. Ms. Andrews, I want to thank you for being here, as well.

The committee is adjourned. Thank you.

[Whereupon, at 4:52 p.m., the subcommittees were adjourned.]

APPENDIX

MATERIAL SUBMITTED FOR THE RECORD

JOINT SUBCOMMITTEE HEARING NOTICE
COMMITTEE ON FOREIGN AFFAIRS
U.S. HOUSE OF REPRESENTATIVES
WASHINGTON, DC 20515-6128

Subcommittee on Terrorism, Nonproliferation, and Trade
Ted Poe (R-TX), Chairman

Subcommittee on the Middle East and North Africa
Ileana Ros-Lehtinen (R-FL), Chairman

TO: MEMBERS OF THE COMMITTEE ON FOREIGN AFFAIRS

You are respectfully requested to attend an OPEN hearing of the Committee on Foreign Affairs, to be held jointly by the Subcommittee on Terrorism, Nonproliferation, and Trade and the Subcommittee on the Middle East and North Africa in Room 2172 of the Rayburn House Office Building (and available live on the Committee website at http://www.ForeignAffairs.house.gov):

DATE: Wednesday, June 18, 2014

TIME: 2:00 p.m.

SUBJECT: The Bergdahl Exchange: Implications for U.S. National Security and the Fight Against Terrorism

WITNESSES: Mr. Andy Andrews
                 Father of deceased Second Lieutenant, USA, Darryn Andrews

                 Spc. Cody Full, USA, Retired
                 (Served with Sgt. Bergdahl in Blackfoot Company, Second Platoon)

                 Mr. Mike Waltz
                 Senior National Security Fellow
                 New America Foundation
                 (Commanded a Special Forces' Company in Eastern Afghanistan in 2009)

                 Mark Jacobson, Ph.D.
                 Senior Advisor
                 Truman National Security Project

By Direction of the Chairman

The Committee on Foreign Affairs seeks to make its facilities accessible to persons with disabilities. If you are in need of special accommodations, please call 202/225-5021 at least four business days in advance of the event, whenever practicable. Questions with regard to special accommodations in general (including availability of Committee materials in alternative formats and assistive listening devices) may be directed to the Committee.

COMMITTEE ON FOREIGN AFFAIRS

MINUTES OF SUBCOMMITTEE ON _Terrorism Nonproliferation and Trade; Middle East and North Africa_ HEARING

Day _Wednesday_ Date _June 18, 2014_ Room _2172_

Starting Time _2:00 p.m._ Ending Time _4:52 p.m._

Recesses | _1_ | (_2:22_ to _2:40_) (___ to ___) (___ to ___) (___ to ___) (___ to ___) (___ to ___)

Presiding Member(s)

Chairman Ted Poe

Check all of the following that apply:

Open Session [✓]   Electronically Recorded (taped) [✓]
Executive (closed) Session [ ]   Stenographic Record [✓]
Televised [✓]

TITLE OF HEARING:

"The Bergdahl Exchange: Implications for U.S. National Security and the Fight Against Terrorism"

SUBCOMMITTEE MEMBERS PRESENT:

Reps. Poe, Ros-Lehtinen, Cotton, Chabot, Kinzinger, Wilson, DeSantis, Meadows, Cook, Yoho, Perry, Duffy, Collins, Weber, Sherman, Cicilline, Connolly, Vargas, Kennedy, Schneider, Frankel, Deutch, and Castro.

NON-SUBCOMMITTEE MEMBERS PRESENT: _(Mark with an * if they are not members of full committee.)_

Rep. Rohrabacher

HEARING WITNESSES: Same as meeting notice attached? Yes [✓] No [ ]
(If "no", please list below and include title, agency, department, or organization.)

STATEMENTS FOR THE RECORD: _(List any statements submitted for the record.)_

Rep. Connolly

TIME SCHEDULED TO RECONVENE _____
or
TIME ADJOURNED _4:52 p.m._

Subcommittee Staff Director

MATERIAL SUBMITTED FOR THE RECORD BY THE HONORABLE TED POE, A REPRESENTA-
TIVE IN CONGRESS FROM THE STATE OF TEXAS, AND CHAIRMAN, SUBCOMMITTEE ON
TERRORISM, NONPROLIFERATION, AND TRADE

From: Erin Lovelady
840 Connecticut Street
Bridge City, TX 77611
409.728.3051

To: Ted Poe
C/o Gina Santucci
2412 Rayburn Building
Washington D.C., 20515

Dear Mr. Poe,

I have contacted you today to express my sadness and anger over the exchange of prisoners that took place this past week; Sgt. Bowe Bergdahl for the five Taliban terrorist. This is especially upsetting to all of my family because when my Dad, Victor Lovelady, was being held hostage a little over a year ago we were told that we "DO NOT NEGOTIATE" with terrorist. The question that continues to come to mind is what makes one American life more important than another and if we are going to negotiate for one, why would you not negotiate for all?

We believe that the only reason that my Dad's story was even reported was thanks to you and your staff. We have also received letters from world leaders with their condolences for the loss of my father. The President and his staff has never addressed our family or even acknowledged that there were three American citizens killed by terrorist last January. During the time my Dad was held hostage it was reported that the terrorist wanted to trade Aafia Siddiqui and Omar Abde-Rahman (Blind Sheik) for the three Americans in the Algerian Gas Facility. The statement from Washington was, "we do not negotiate with terrorist." What has changed now that we are allowing to free terrorist that are convicted of war crimes and murder?

Mr. Poe, please continue to fight for all Americans that have been affected by terrorism. The President and his staff should be held accountable for the release of these five terrorist. The only thing that has been accomplished with their release is condemning more American Soldiers and civilians in the United States and abroad to death at the hands of terrorist.

Thank you for your representation for Texas and the United States of America.

With gratitude,

Erin Lovelady
Daughter of Victor Lovelady
Killed January 17, 2013 at the In Amenas Gas Facility

81

Congressman Poe,

I want to express my total disgust for the exchange of prisoners that took place this past week; Sgt. Bowe Bergdahl for five Taliban terrorists. Sadly, this weakens our country and hits especially close to home for me and my family because of the circumstances my brother, Victor Lovelady, endured after being captured by and his death at the hands of terrorists in Algeria. I dare say that without you and Randy Weber the world would not have known about the three Americans that were killed in the raid on the gas plant in Algeria.

During my brother's capture it was reported that the terrorists wanted to trade Aafia Siddiqui and Omar Abde-Rahman (Blind Sheik) for the three Americans. The statement from Washington was,"we do not negotiate with terrorists."

Please keep the pressure on the President and his staff and be sure they are held accountable for the release of these five hardened terrorists that will undoubtedly resurface and kill Americans either in the United States or abroad.

Thank you for your representation for Texas and the United States of America.

Sincerely,

Michael Lovelady
2308 Franklin Avenue
Nederland, Texas   77627

409-719-8175

Statement for the Record from Rep. Connolly
The Bergdahl Exchange: Implications for
U.S. National Security and the Fight Against Terrorism
Joint Subcommittee Hearing: Subcommittee on Terrorism, Nonproliferation, and Trade,
Subcommittee on the Middle East and North Africa
2:00 PM, Wednesday, June 18, 2014

Mr. Andrews, I would first like to offer my deepest sympathies to you and your family for the loss of your son, Second Lieutenant, USA, Darryn Andrews. The families of fallen American soldiers bear a terrible burden. They witness their loved ones raise their right hand, knowing that military service will undoubtedly put them in harm's way, while praying for their safe return that ultimately does not come.

Mr. Chairman, today I hope we can honor the memory of Second Lieutenant Andrews by providing his father a venue to offer testimony to both his son's bravery and the cost of war. Witness accounts state that Second Lieutenant Andrews was killed in action pushing his fellow soldiers out of the way of an incoming RPG, an incredible act of gallantry. His selflessness was unqualified and his actions without hesitation.

Mr. Andrews is here today to bear witness to the sorrow of a father who lost his son on the battlefield, and only he can articulate those raw emotions. I wish we provided each of 4,486 families who lost loved ones in Iraq and the 2,331 families who lost loved ones in Afghanistan an opportunity to honor the memory of their fallen soldiers before this Congress and the country. I think we would find that all death in war is tragic and underscores the importance of this Committee, the Congress, and the Administration's pursuit of diplomatic resolutions to global conflicts.

The issue before this Committee today is the Administration's decision to exchange Sergeant Bowe Bergdahl, an American soldier held in captivity for nearly five years, for five Guantanamo Bay detainees. Our discussion should help us evaluate the impact of the exchange on national security and the fight against terrorism, but we should be careful not to play the role of judge and jury in litigating Sgt. Bergdahl's service record.

Heroic figure or not, we must agree that Sgt. Bergdahl should be afforded the full rights of an American soldier. The "no service member left behind" axiom that the President and Secretary of Defense sought to uphold in seeking terms for Sgt. Bergdahl's release is sacred in our armed services. At no point has the United States deemed Sgt. Bergdahl undeserving of this standard. It is my hope that this Committee does not use this hearing to make qualitative statements about Sgt. Bergdahl's service record and supplant the due process to which he and every American soldier are entitled.

What we know, is that Sgt. Bergdahl vanished from his guard post on June 30, 2009 while serving with the 501st Parachute Infantry Regiment in Afghanistan and later fell into the hands of the Haqqani network. The day after his disappearance, the Pentagon classified him as "duty status whereabouts unknown" and subsequently initiated a search mission, DUSTWUN, termed for Sgt. Bergdahl's classification. Two days later, Sgt. Bergdahl was listed as "missing-captured," a classification he retained for the duration of his captivity.

Sgt. Bergdahl's parents and the outside world only learned of his condition while in captivity through direct and indirect talks between the U.S. and his captors, written correspondence and sporadically released videos. His parents' anguish and torment were undoubtedly hanging on each intermittent communication that they received. Especially, as they witnessed the physical condition of their son deteriorate from years of living in captivity. Leading up to the exchange, Pentagon officials certified that Sgt. Bergdahl's condition rendered the effort to secure his release urgent if they hoped to bring him home alive. Sgt. Bergdahl's health has been cited as a reason the Administration did not provide notice to Congress 30 days before transferring the Guantanamo Bay detainees as required by statute in the National Defense Authorization Act. Secretary of Defense Hagel conceded last Thursday at a hearing before the House Armed Services Committee that the Administration could have done a better job of keeping Congress informed, and I believe the issue of Congressional notification in this case warrants further evaluation.

The ultimate arrangement that brought Sgt. Bergdahl home was negotiated through indirect talks with the Taliban administered by the Government of Qatar. These talks began after negotiations between the U.S. and the Taliban faltered in March 2012. Some have cited the structure of the talks and the parties involved in questioning whether or not the U.S. negotiated with terrorists for Sgt. Bergdahl's release. Rather than taking this overly juridical approach, I believe a sober discussion about the kaleidoscope of hostile groups that our soldiers encounter on the modern battlefield and how that impacts our approach to retrieving captured American soldiers would be more valuable. Further, now that a deal has been reached, we must look to how the U.S. can ensure that the five former detainees do not return to the battlefield and inflict harm upon American soldiers and our allies.

I am disheartened that the issue of Sgt. Bergdahl's exchange has become the source of political theater for Congress when serious issues surrounding the deal remain unexamined. I have witnessed my colleagues question the severity of Sgt. Bergdahl's health issues and the sincerity of the military doctors attempting to treat him. The suggestion that Sgt. Bergdahl's actions, whatever they may have been, warranted that he should have remained with the Taliban in perpetuity is reprehensible. It is my hope that we can separate the questions surrounding the Bergdahl exchange into those that merit a fair hearing before this Congress, those that should be left to the courts, and those that deserve our utmost contempt.

www.ingramcontent.com/pod-product-compliance
Lightning Source LLC
Chambersburg PA
CBHW081844280526
45789CB00007B/2557